CONTENTMENT
Unravelled

Exploring the Realms of True Fulfillment

Copyright © 2025 Markey Writing Academy CONTENTMENT UNRAVELLED

First published by Markey Writing Academy 2025.

Find us on Facebook @KellyMarkeyAuthor, Instagram @Author_Kelly_Markey and LinkedIn @kellymarkey

Paperback ISBN: 978-1-7636837-3-0   E-Book ISBN: 978-1-7636837-4-7

The right of Kelly Markey to be identified as the author of this work has been asserted in accordance with the Copyright Amendment (Moral Rights) Act 2000.

This work is copyright. The Book/Ebook contains material which is owned by or licensed to me, the author of the Book/Ebook. This material includes, but is not limited to the design, layout, look, appearance and graphics marked©. Reproduction is prohibited other than in accordance with the copyright notice, which forms part of these terms and conditions.

DISCLAIMER – The content of the pages of this Book/Ebook is for general information and use only. It is subject to change without notice.

The author takes no responsibility or liability for the use of any theories, strategies or methods that might be used in verbal or practical applications.

All rights reserved. No part of this publication may be reproduced, stored in or introduced into a retrieval system, or transmitted in any form, or by any means (electronic, mechanical, photocopying, recording or otherwise) without the prior written permission of the author. Any person who does any unauthorised act in relation to this publication may be liable to criminal prosecution and civil claims for damages. Enquiries should be made to the publisher.

Cover Design: Markey Writing Academy
Layout: Markey Writing Academy
Typesetting: Markey Writing Academy

Markey Writing Academy
Central Coast New South Wales,
Australia 2250
www.kellymarkey.com

Table of Contents

Praise for The Book ~~~~~~~~~~~~~~~~~~~~~~~~~~~~~~~~~~ 2

Other Books by Kelly Markey ~~~~~~~~~~~~~~~~~~~~~~~~~ 6

Publisher's Preface ~~~~~~~~~~~~~~~~~~~~~~~~~~~~~~~~~ 8

Foreword ~~~~~~~~~~~~~~~~~~~~~~~~~~~~~~~~~~~~~~~ 10

Introduction ~~~~~~~~~~~~~~~~~~~~~~~~~~~~~~~~~~~~~ 12

The Gist of Life ~~~~~~~~~~~~~~~~~~~~~~~~~~~~~~~~~~ 17

Superficial Satisfaction ~~~~~~~~~~~~~~~~~~~~~~~~~~~~~ 25

Complications to Contentment ~~~~~~~~~~~~~~~~~~~~~~~~ 35

Finding your Equilibrium ~~~~~~~~~~~~~~~~~~~~~~~~~~~ 44

Habits for Satisfaction ~~~~~~~~~~~~~~~~~~~~~~~~~~~~~ 54

Contentment Does Not Stem from Fame and Fortune ~~~~~~~~~ 54

Practice Prepares You for Success ~~~~~~~~~~~~~~~~~~~~~ 65

Expectation Versus Reality ~~~~~~~~~~~~~~~~~~~~~~~~~~ 73

Craft the Right Attitude ~~~~~~~~~~~~~~~~~~~~~~~~~~~~ 85

The Correlation Between Happiness and Contentment ~~~~~~~~ 95

The Benefits of Contentment ~~~~~~~~~~~~~~~~~~~~~~~~ 102

Attaining Contentment ~~~~~~~~~~~~~~~~~~~~~~~~~~~~ 114

Pathways to True Contentment ~~~~~~~~~~~~~~~~~~~~~~ 123

Conquered Contentment ~~~~~~~~~~~~~~~~~~~~~~~~~~~ 130

About the Author ~~~~~~~~~~~~~~~~~~~~~~~~~~~~~~~ 139

Celebrating Literary Excellence ~~~~~~~~~~~~~~~~~~~~~~ 140

Markey Writing Academy ~~~~~~~~~~~~~~~~~~~~~~~~~~ 142

Beacon of Hope Mission ~~~~~~~~~~~~~~~~~~~~~~~~~~~ 143

Beacon of Hope Mission Forum ~~~~~~~~~~~~~~~~~~~~~~ 144

Beacon of Hope Awards ~~~~~~~~~~~~~~~~~~~~~~~~~~~ 145

Top Book of the Year ~~~~~~~~~~~~~~~~~~~~~~~~~~~~~ 147

Featured on the New York Times Square Billboard ~~~~~~~~~~ 148

Acknowledgments~~~~~~149

Reference~~~~~~150

Notes

Praise for The Book

First came Oprah Winfrey, the pronounced, then Dr. Phil, and now there's you. This impeccable book shows us how to craft a life of wonder by embracing hurdles and challenges. It gives us the opportunity to learn from lived experience and find inspiration in all fabrics of life.

Fox News

In a world that often feels overwhelmed by the rush for success and validation, Kelly Markey's *Contentment Unravelled* offers a profound and timely reminder to slow down, reflect, and recalibrate. This book goes beyond simply advocating for self-respect and emotional well-being; it serves as an invitation to explore our personal values, relationships, and the way we handle life's challenges.

Markey's voice is at the forefront of the book, candidly sharing her personal experiences and perspectives with conviction. *Contentment Unravelled* offers deeply personal reflections on resilience, self-love, and the pursuit of a balanced life, instead of focusing on universal truths. This approach allows the book to invite readers into a more individualized exploration of contentment, making its insights feel relatable and authentic to each person's unique journey. The author's vulnerability draws readers into her world as she explores themes like boundaries, emotional landscapes, and the transformative power of self-respect.

One of the most compelling aspects of *Contentment Unravelled* is view of self-love as an ongoing, active process, rather than a static state. Markey emphasizes that self-love isn't just about celebrating our strengths, but also about confronting our vulnerabilities. She encourages readers to look inward, peel back layers of doubt and fear, and emerge with a renewed sense of purpose and authenticity.

What sets *Contentment Unravelled* apart is Markey's unapologetic stance on self-respect. She argues that self-respect is non-negotiable, demonstrating how standing firm in one's values – even when uncomfortable – is essential for personal growth. This emphasis on setting and maintaining boundaries resonates deeply in today's emotionally charged world, where navigating difficult relationships and making peace with past traumas are ongoing challenges.

The book also explores faith and spirituality, offering a lens through which to view peace, acceptance, and transformation. Markey's use of Biblical references adds an additional layer of depth, but the book's insights are universally relatable, appealing to readers regardless of their belief system.

Markey's introspective yet declarative writing style can sometimes feel more like a monologue than a dialogue, but this singular approach gives the book its potency. Her unflinching candour challenges readers to reconsider their perspectives, even if they don't always agree with every viewpoint.

Ultimately, the most powerful takeaway from *Contentment Unravelled* is its hopeful message.

Markey reminds us that contentment is not about perfection, but about progress. It's about finding joy in small victories and viewing setbacks as opportunities for growth, not failures. She urges us to embrace life's imperfections, recognizing them as essential parts of the journey toward wholeness.

For readers seeking a personal and reflective exploration of life's complexities, *Contentment Unravelled* provides a valuable framework for understanding the delicate balance between our inner lives and the external world. Markey's work challenges us to rethink how we define and pursue happiness, offering a perspective that is both deeply rooted and open to interpretation.

In the end, Kelly Markey's *Contentment Unravelled* is a powerful reminder that, while contentment may not come easily, it is always worth striving for. Through her words, readers are encouraged to embrace resilience, honour self-respect, and live authentically.

Stephanie Tranquille, Director, speakerstephspeak.

As a painter strokes their canvas with colour, Kelly's kaleidoscope of word use will tantalise readers' creative written word desires.

Kelly has approached the state of contentment with her word flair that envelopes her readers into connecting with the various states that one desires. I found reading about well-known people from around the world sharing their stories about where they found contentment insightful and a clever use of moments to highlight this pursued state. As Kelly herself generously opened up about her times of fear and grief that fell on her like a deluge of sorrow, she looked to the simplest things to find gratitude and appreciation, which held her in moments of contentment. How fragile contentment can be if not seized. And how quickly it can elude us if we are not open to grasping and relaxing in the moment. Everyone walks a single path with many facets, and our journeys for moments of contentment are all unique.

Contentment Unravelled is the perfect sequel to Kelly's previous books written on making decisions, motivation, her brother's suicide and society's part that contributed to this tragedy, and her personal story.

As I read the manuscript, Kelly Markey's written words pulled me along, allowing me to complete pages with ease. I also liked her use of statistics and references to nature.

This book is my favourite... so far. Kelly Markey is a storyteller, and I'm sure she will include more truths from herself and collective stories in anthologies to be released. Thank you for sharing your wisdom.

Janice Morris Author, An Educator's Handbook and Echoes of Humanity: Anthology, published by Markey Writing Academy

The messages in this book are profound. It really resonates with me. This book is going to be another great addition to the body of high-impact literature. I salute you for sharing these great nuggets! I appreciate how you have woven personal anecdotes, life stories, and actual research into the book.

Dr. Stephanie, Songwriter and Author

A literary masterpiece that dares to unravel the soul Kelly Markey's *Contentment Unravelled* isn't just a book; it's a mirror, a map, and a mentor rolled into one. It holds the kind of wisdom that stirs your spirit and shakes the foundations of your assumptions about life, happiness, and fulfillment.

From the opening lines, Markey's unfiltered candour captures your attention, weaving personal anecdotes with timeless truths. Her writing isn't merely a call to self-reflection – it's a challenge to confront the chaos, own your vulnerabilities, and redefine what it means to live authentically. Each page is an invitation to abandon societal expectations and instead embrace a deeper understanding of resilience, self-respect, and grace.

One of the book's most compelling aspects is its reframing of contentment. Markey paints it not as a passive state of happiness but as an active, ongoing process of discovery, acceptance, and growth. Through vivid storytelling and profound reflections, she bridges the gap between life's chaos and the peace that comes with intentionality. Whether discussing boundaries, self-love, or navigating adversity, she leaves readers not just inspired but equipped.

Markey's bold, unapologetic emphasis on self-respect and the power of boundaries is particularly timely. In an age of emotional turbulence and relational complexities, her message is a lifeline. By challenging readers to stand firm in their values, she offers a transformative blueprint for living a life grounded in authenticity.

The book also ventures into the often-unspoken realms of faith and spirituality, layering universal truths with practical tools. Her words resonate across belief systems, appealing to anyone who seeks meaning beyond material success. Markey's ability to intertwine biblical wisdom with personal experiences adds depth without alienating readers of different backgrounds.

Yet, *Contentment Unravelled* is not for the faint of heart. It demands honesty, introspection, and action. Markey doesn't sugarcoat life's struggles – she shines a light on them, encouraging readers to find beauty in the brokenness. Her words challenge you to rethink the way you approach setbacks, urging you to see them as opportunities for growth rather than obstacles.

Ultimately, the true power of this book lies in its ability to transform. It isn't a passive read; it's a journey. Each chapter pushes you closer to the realization that contentment isn't about perfection – it's about progress. It's about embracing life's imperfections and learning to live fully in the present.

Markey's *Contentment Unravelled* is a masterclass in the art of living intentionally. It's the kind of book that doesn't just sit on your shelf-it changes how you see the world, your choices, and yourself. For anyone yearning for clarity, balance, or a sense of purpose, this is your guide.

Carlos Siqueira, Top Motivational Speaker, Business Acceleration Strategist, and Founder of GetOnMoreStages.Com

Other Books by Kelly Markey
Award-Winning and Bestselling Author

Don't Just Fly, SOAR

The inspiration and tools you need to rise above adversity and create a life by design

Glean, Grow, and Glow

Timeless journal to celebrate your growth journey

Legacy Playbook

Unearthing eternal echoes and unveiling the tapestry of legacy

Making Sage Decisions

Mastering the art of decision-making, sculpting choices, and taming the brute within so you can usher forth a better world

The Life of Jayandra

Death is a certainty for us all, so why have we not mastered grief and living authentically? This is a narrative that transcends beyond the shadows of suicide.

Echoes of Humanity (co-author and curated)

Exploring human wonders through the pages of Lessons, Afflictions, Distress, Triumph, Victory, and Brilliance

Publisher's Preface

These significant eye-openers are worth integrating into your character. I have made a magnificent effort to provide you with a set of focused principles for the seldom-travelled road to contentment. *Contentment Unravelled* is Kelly Markey's magnum opus, the summation of my lived experiences and study of contentment. With this book, Kelly Markey secured her stance in the position of prominence in unravelling contentment. My candour in this book is not just to highlight how we get bogged down but also to emphasise how to reach a path to authentic contentment. Contentment is not about attaining your ambitions. It is about aligning your goals with your values. Advancement void of purpose is unfulfilling. Achievement without influence is fading. Triumph is most satisfying when it obliges the people and morals that matter to you. In the banquet of your heart, there are two paths – one for your contentment and the other for your perpetual yearning. You get to decide which one you will travel on.

In an age defined by relentless pursuit and fleeting satisfaction, *Contentment Unravelled* emerges as a beacon of insight and inspiration. As a bestselling and award-winning author, Founder & CEO of the Beacon of Hope Mission and the Markey Writing Academy, I have witnessed firsthand the transformative power of genuine contentment. This book invites readers to explore the profound essence of what it means to be truly content in a world often overshadowed by external pressures.

Through personal anecdotes, deep reflections, and practical wisdom, this work delves into the intricate layers of contentment, challenging conventional beliefs and revealing the profound peace that arises from embracing our authentic selves. It is a journey of self-discovery, underscoring the importance of gratitude, presence, and the richness of everyday experiences.

I wrote *Contentment Uravelled* because I have witnessed firsthand the relentless pursuit of happiness that often leaves people feeling empty rather than fulfilled. In a world that equates success with material wealth, status and external validation, I have seen how easily contentment slips through our fingers, no matter how much we achieve. Through my own journey – marked by trials, triumphs and deep introspection – I realised that true fulfillment does not lie in what we acquire but in who we become. This book is an invitation to peel back the layers of societal expectations and self-imposed pressures to explore the essence of lasting contentment and to embrace a life of true inner peace.

As you turn the pages, I encourage you to reflect on your own life and to consider what it means to find lasting joy amid life's complexities. *Contentment Unravelled* is not just a guide; it's an invitation to cultivate a deeper understanding of happiness and fulfillment. I am honoured to present this work, which I believe will resonate with anyone seeking to uncover the true essence of contentment.

Kelly Markey
CEO & Founder, Markey Writing Academy
International Bestselling & Award-Winning Author
CEO & Founder, Beacon of Hope Mission
Global Award-Winning Publisher
Brand Ambassador for HOPE
Featured on New York Times Square Billboard

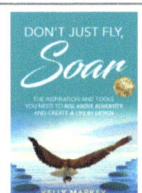     

If you are looking to advance your business or personal portfolio:
Make Sage Decisions, Advocate for Social Justice, Ambassador of Hope, Craft Resilience, Suicide Awareness and Navigate Discrimination, **I am your Maven!**
Author, Speaker, Change Maker, Business Pundit, Facilitator, Subject Matter Expert, Corporate Coach and Publisher

Foreword

A few years ago, at an event bustling with activity and inspiring individuals, my attention was inexplicably drawn to a figure of quiet grace and humility – Kelly Markey. Her poise was not just visual; it resonated with a humility that spoke volumes. That evening sparked a curiosity and desire in me to connect with her. Little did I know, our paths were divinely set to intersect.

Several months later, she asked me a question at another event where I was a panellist. As soon as she spoke, I recognised her and felt an immediate kinship – an innate sense of belonging to the same tribe. This meeting marked the beginning of a deep and enduring friendship, much beyond professional platforms.

Kelly Markey, an acclaimed international best-selling author and visionary, stands as a beacon of hope and a force for transformative social change. As the CEO and Founder of Markey Writing Academy and Beacon of Hope, Kelly's commitment to uplifting narratives and empowering voices is profound and unparalleled.

In *Contentment Unravelled*, Kelly invites us on a journey exploring the many dimensions of contentment through her encounters and challenges. Her genius in writing is evident as she poses thought-provoking questions, urging readers to delve deep into understanding what it truly means to be content.

Kelly shares, *"I wrote this book from my heart and lived experience. Everything within these pages comes from my interpretations, residual knowledge, and personal beliefs. I have spent an enormous amount of time researching and reading to unearth concrete evidence about contentment."* In an age marked by relentless pursuit and often unattainable ideals, contentment is portrayed as a quiet rebellion against the noise of dissatisfaction. For Kelly, Contentment Unravelled signifies the journey of peeling back layers of societal expectations, revealing the profound peace that comes from embracing the present moment.

This book intricately explores the relationship between personal fulfilment and societal pressures, offering insights and tools to cultivate a deeper sense of gratitude and acceptance. Through sharing stories and reflections, Kelly aims to inspire readers to redefine success and happiness on their terms, fostering a collective movement towards a more harmonious and compassionate existence for all.

Reflecting on my understanding of contentment, rooted in my Christian faith, I recall the lessons from my childhood in a rural village. Despite the apparent lack of material resources, I experienced a profound level of contentment grounded in a loving and supportive home environment, a deep connection to my faith, and a life lived on purpose. My mother often cited the scripture, *"Godliness with contentment is great gain,"* guiding me to seek lasting contentment instead of fleeting desires. These foundations enabled me to weather many storms and scale numerous mountains, all while maintaining inner peace. It is precisely the form of contentment Kelly illuminates.

Kelly Markey's insights appreciate the delicate balance between embracing contentment and avoiding complacency. She warns against the dangers of lingering in the comfort zone and pursuing superficial desires, emphasising the need for intentional dreaming rooted in true purpose. It resonates deeply with my approach to transformational coaching, where I inspire individuals to tap into their infinite potential through the divine spirit that guides them.

In our shared vision, living a life of intention means not leaving things to chance but actively crafting a direction. As Kelly eloquently puts it, allowing life to collide with probabilities while becoming adept at managing risks transforms how we experience contentment – it becomes something that we embody and live, salvaged by intention. Kelly Markey highlights a universal truth: no matter what stage of life we find ourselves in or the challenges we face, contentment is accessible to all. With the right mindset and a laser-focused intention deeply rooted in faith, each of us can achieve and dwell in this profound state of contentment.

Her message underscores that contentment isn't a distant destination but a place we can inhabit daily through conscious choices and mindful living. It aligns seamlessly with my commitment to helping individuals live expansive lives, utilising the infinite power bestowed by the divine spirit. I wholeheartedly join Kelly in encouraging a journey towards authenticity and intentionality. I urge readers to get honest about what they observe, dream of, pursue, and contribute to. By doing so, we foster a life where contentment is not just an outcome but a continuous, empowering process.

Prepare yourself for an enthralling experience. As you turn the pages of *Contentment Unravelled*, you will be inspired to look beyond the superficiality of temporary satisfaction and glimpse the essence of genuine contentment. Kelly encourages us to dwell in a spiritual state of contentment, no matter the circumstances, thereby transforming our understanding of what it means to truly *"be content."*

May the weary soul find solace and a blueprint within these pages to navigate life's twists and turns and eventually arrive at the worthy destination of true contentment.

Dr. Stephanie Fletcher-Lartey
Transformation Coach,
Director: Arete Professional Consulting
Head: Marketplace Missions Movement Global

Introduction

The birth of this book started with many seasons of excruciating life challenges, an affliction that hovered with no pause. Both family and friends were deemed qualified to diagnose a remedy served on a silver platter-making assumptions on so many fronts. Living in this vortex that serves up restlessness and weariness in proportions that no one can tame. I had to reach a place of CONTENTMENT to navigate this one audacious life. I had to introspect and decide who to let into my world of influence. I had to learn to be satisfied with what I had. I had to learn how to walk away from people who did not champion my welfare but pretended by default to care about me. I had to dig deep to find a source of contentment that would not deplete me and unravel renewed innovations of refinement and gratitude. I marinated with this, found my balance, and assured contentment that I live in thought, deed, and action. Sustaining contentment is a craft, and this book delves into this craftsmanship.

Human life is the highest expression of civilisation. We are at the apex of the grand food chain. Yet our behaviours, characteristics, and emotions do not always pave the way to showcase our development. We rarely evaluate our actions and mindsets to enhance our moral conduct. When you live with an authentic motto, you can zoom into every facet of your moral compass and align it strategically. Genuineness is about being unfiltered. It's about actual values that you live up to and turn every rock to find YOUR CONTENTMENT. The target is not to fight every battle and win each war but rather to see what tugs your heartstrings and how to flow in with the power to glow consistently. As you wander in the terrain of life, take obligatory time to comprehend, appreciate, understand, realise, grow, escalate, grasp, smell, stagnate, mourn, cry, laugh, and smile. Just like there are ample routes that rivers meander into the sea, there are sufficient ways to soar to the summits of contentment. Some of my expressions are highlighted in this book through my lived experience and acquired knowledge and insight.

Craft a persona to starve your distractions and feed your focus. The principle of trigger and consequence is that, in essence, you reap what you sow. If you dispense love and respect freely, this will most definitely be returned to you. The wellspring of creation, your thoughts, deeds, and actions will dictate your future. Whatever you manifest will craft your future with precision. The value of humility is priceless, especially when you need to humble yourself and assess your current reality based on your past actions, choices, and lack of contentment. The attitude of growth ignites from within, which is directly correlated to your perpetual level of contentment-the one thing you can genuinely **CONTROL BY YOURSELF.** The norm of focusing on everything that comes hurling your way unravels the defined plan. Seek the stimulant that stirs up your serenity instead-zoom into your core values. The belief in endurance and compensation is etched in consistency, which is the first cousin of contentment. When your actions consistently match your words, then you will see rewards for your character, which will be converted to contentment.

Don't embroil yourself in a predicament to betray yourself. The stance of change is such that history will repeat itself until you learn the lessons and implement change to halt the cycle. Alteration gives you a new conduit to crack open yourself to candid delight, realisation, and improvement. The origin of integrity traces back to The Merriam-Webster Dictionary, which dates this word back to the 14th century and defines it as:

- "Firm adherence to a code of especially moral or artistic values: INCORRUPTIBILITY
- An unimpaired condition: SOUNDNESS
- The quality or state of being complete or undivided: COMPLETENESS."

When you purposely live your life with fundamental integrity, then you will find contentment pumping in your veins. Authentic happiness activates when you can genuinely look in the mirror and be content with who you are. Never live in a place where you must haggle your sense of integrity. You must master some degree of success with integrity if your purpose is to find contentment.

Don't compromise who you are and expect the world to roll out the red carpet for you. The pillars of character that will compromise your contentment are morality, ethics, integrity, discretion, professionalism, principles, values, and loyalty. The accurate opportunity for contentment lies within you and how you craft your character. Just as gold is purified to remove all the impurities, you need to purify your character to be certified as a rare commodity. Strength does not come from ignoring flaws. It stems from self-awareness of what does not work well in your life and moving towards alignment for true contentment. Contentment is forged in the fortitude to persevere towards an acceptable remedy. Contentment is not the absence of hardship; it is navigating difficulties and building resilience while you find your true north.

Refrain from sitting with and dwelling in sponsored and self-crafted sympathy. Instead, hone in on the immense WHY factor, what energises you and depletes you, who honours you and disregards you. Define what success means to you and how you paint failure. What encapsulates your significance? The most excellent driver to contentment is to leave a significant legacy that will surge through the progression of time. Are you intentional about your level of achievement and contentment? Ancient wisdom and modern innovation-have you struck your balance in the contentment gauge? What resonates with you as a song of contentment? Some things will always be completely out of your hands. Grasp what you can control and what you cannot, and therein lie the fundamentals for contentment. It would be best if you find peace precisely where you are, even when the stars are not shimmering amidst the timing you did not bargain for. Even in the eye of the storm when your strength is depleted.

This book is enshrined with the competence, confidence, and acumen you need to unravel your contentment and seal it with zeal. We assume that contentment is our birthright, but very few of us remember to cultivate it. In general nature, humans are effervescent in their quest for more all the time. Man is seldom satisfied with what he possesses and frequently feels a lack of contentment. Granted that as a species, we own the insufficiency of earthly goods and superficial connection. Yet we never really ponder on assets that genuinely increase the level of contentment: authentic connection and eternal assets. Have you discerned the difference between temporal things and the exponential growth and approaching change? Change towards what ultimately matters when the final trumpet shall sound. Dissatisfaction frequently arises from a sense of yearning rather than an optimistic distress. We are subject to vanity and the bondage of so many lofty things. Fluctuation is the fad fashion rather than finding an anchor of satisfaction in any given circumstance.

Those chickens will begin to come home to roost, when you are unconscious to the unconcerned tune that lurks into the vicissitudes of life. When you refuse to focus on the micro things that affect the landscape of your life in profound ways, you covet what you do not have and lack appreciation for what you do have. It is the recipe for disappointment. Everything has a shelf life: your wealth, your health, your body, your spirituality, your relationships, and your time on earth. Everyone has their peculiar idiosyncrasies; however, the commonality that unites us is the fact that we all have bitter regrets, which sometimes can never be restored. We have all created our yardstick to measure how people perform in our lives or refuse to, so our level of contentment is related to expectations that are beyond our control. You put your happiness in someone else's hand. Your bubble of contentment is in danger when in the vicinity of others. This book will unravel to you how to nurture your nest of contentment and build it on a firm foundation that will stand the test of time.

It is impossible to cultivate a gratified character when you concentrate on only visible objects. To revoke the heart from outward objects and lift it to those things that offer better securities, viz: faith, love, compassion, and reliability, is among the things that result in endeavours toward happiness. True contentment is not found in yet another indispensable attainment. What you do on your bad day is what counts rather than what you do on good days-standing in your ruins long enough to learn and realign towards something far superior. You can choose from the charcuterie board of life. As you stroll through this book, may your heart, soul, and mind ignite with new possibilities. May it kindle epiphanies that you can implement in your life to move towards a superior level of contentment. *"Employ your time in improving yourself by other men's writing, so that you shall gain easily what others have labelled hard for."* – Socrates. Enjoy the read and the fundamental gleanings.

I wrote this book from my heart and lived experience. Everything within these pages comes from my interpretations, residual knowledge, and personal beliefs. In addition, I have spent an enormous amount of time researching and reading to unearth concrete evidence about contentment. In an age marked by relentless pursuit and often unattainable ideals, contentment emerges as a quiet rebellion against the noise of dissatisfaction. To me, *Contentment Unravelled* signifies the journey of peeling back layers of societal expectations, revealing the profound peace that comes from embracing the present moment. This book explores the intricate relationship between personal fulfilment and societal pressures, offering insights and tools to cultivate a deeper sense of gratitude and acceptance. By sharing stories and reflections, I aim to inspire readers to redefine success and happiness on their terms, fostering a collective movement towards a more harmonious and compassionate existence for all.

In exploring the art of contentment, I uncover the erudite and rational insights that challenge conventional notions of happiness. Contentment is not merely the absence of desire but a profound understanding of one's place in the world. This book invites you to engage with your thoughts critically, discerning between fleeting wants and lasting fulfillment. Through introspection and mindfulness, you can unravel the complexities of your aspirations, recognising that true contentment lies in acceptance and gratitude for what you have. This book aims to provide a framework for cultivating this state of being, encouraging readers to embrace simplicity and authenticity, ultimately leading to a more balanced and meaningful life.

I am not afraid of death…it will not be my first choice, though…

C – O – N – T – E – N – T – M – E – N – T is most definitely my first choice. We all have our desires delegated into the frame of our existence. Are you confident that you are part of the most magnificent glistening? People who will not change are famous for telling a sad tale. This book invites you on a journey to graft, toil, and refine your uber-precious sentiments toward the fine art of contentment. The cause and effect of your decisions and deeds will eventually manifest in all facets of life. *"To be yourself in a world that is constantly trying to make you something else is the greatest accomplishment. For the world makes way for the man who knows where he is going."* – Ralph Waldo Emerson. Have you ever pondered your destination? What encapsulates your authentic contentment? The toughest people that I have encountered have navigated through harsh conditions. They learned to construct strength and contentment from gloomy places. **"Contentment is natural wealth; luxury is artificial poverty."** – Socrates.

The Gist of Life

Life has no undisputed blueprint. We are all trying to find a way and what ultimately brings us true happiness. Even if your life has reached the giddy heights of grandeur, with polished accolades in every facet-why do you still feel unsatisfied at times? Have you genuinely introspected your life? What is the gist of life? To wander around each day until someday, the compass strikes a direction to something. Are you currently living a fulfilled life? Are you living an authentic life? Do you live in a façade? Have you eliminated all traces of frustration, mediocrity, and hassles from your life? *"Our greatest fear should not be a failure, but of succeeding at things in life that don't really matter."* – Francis Chan. Do you understand what matters in your life – what makes your heart sing?

In all its splendour, life is delightful in default mode. Most of us have the basic needs to sustain us; things get complicated when we seek external complexities. The fundamentals of food, clothing, and shelter do not cut the mustard. We have evolved to foster greater expectations, and not all of us are as resourceful as others to meet our ambitious hopes. You may be born to the same parents and have the same opportunities, but your life is different from your sibling's. Why? Have you passively converted your aspirations to responsibilities? Have you objectively asked yourself how this happened? Why did you allow your dreams and hopes to vanish?

Contentment is universal. People around the globe from every demographic and age are on a quest to find happiness within themselves, careers, marriage, finance, networks, countries, and, sadly, social media. Have you attained true happiness? With reference to the dictionary, happiness is described as *"a state of being happy."* Unfortunately, we cannot order this *"state"* online; update your status, maybe. Conjure it up-no. It is the opposite of sadness. Happiness is **a sense of well-being, joy, or contentment.** When people are successful, safe, or favoured, they feel happiness. The *"pursuit of happiness"* is something this life is based on, and different people feel happiness for various reasons. With reference to the Bible, Psalm 37:3-4, *"Delight yourself in the Lord, and he will give you the desires of your heart."* This verse not only commands us to trust the Lord but reminds us that finding delight in the Lord will also result in positive things coming your way.

What is happiness according to the Bible? It's an attitude of the heart and spirit, often synonymous with but not limited to following Jesus Christ and pursuing a Christian life. *"But the fruit of the Spirit is love, joy, peace, patience, kindness, goodness, faithfulness, gentleness, and self-control; against such things there is no law."* Your definition of happiness may be different, yet we all have the same desire to fulfil. It's impossible to put the genie in the bottle; be strategic about understanding and unleashing your driving force towards contentment. From a selection criterion of qualitative and quantitative analysis, what exists in spades in your life: peace, joy, laughter, pain, tears, bitterness, contentment, or anxiety?

Are you in a rat race? Do you get up with no zeal? Do you meander through each day without absolute determination? Are you driven by purpose? Do you struggle to admit mistakes to yourself and others? By spiteful decree, do you hide from others and yourself because dealing with the truth is just too complicated? Have you discovered the purpose of your life? Do you have a bona fide proof that your initial understanding was correct? Success does not equate to happiness. Wealth certainly does not denote contentment. What congruence undergirds the hazards of your contentment: do you leave things to chance, let life collide with probabilities, craft a direction, and are you skilled at managing risks? Do you know how to wear contentment on your skin, heart, and soul salvaged by intention? *"Patience, persistence, and perspiration make an unbeatable combination for success."* – Napoleon Hill. Is this your ladder? Refrain from existing like you are endangered or disappearing while you are living. Get authentic about the things you observe, dream of, pursue, contribute to, provide, feel, support, ignore, shove under the carpet, acquire, develop, procure, rob, steal, and expect.

These behaviours set the tone and narrative of contentment. Remove yourself from all distractions and get genuine with yourself: what has brought you shame and honour in bountiful measure? Refinements, certainties, benefits, cruelty, inductions, encouragements, adjustments, disrespect, loyalty, trust, betrayal, scepticism, doubt, mistrust, and advancements. What view has your life painted to date? Are you proud and happy with how your life is? We all have confrontation wounds from the festival of life; we gain these by hiding our genuine emotions and masking our level of joy. It eventually corrodes our bandwidth of contentment. You will never lavish contentment if you wear the aroma of a victim. Every single day, the universe delivers evidence that the world is collaborating to either make us cheerful or glum; take your pick. *"Keep your face always towards the sunshine, and shadows will fall behind you."* – Unknown.

South Africa has many indigenous tribes. Each tribe has a national emblem. During a cultural tour in Africa, I was fascinated by the logic and explanation of why each tribe chose a certain totem. The Royal Bafokeng is the ethnic homeland of the Bafokeng people, a Setswana-speaking traditional community. Most Setswana tribes, like other South African tribes, have an animal that symbolises the nation. The crocodile is the genealogical totem of the Basotho-Batswana people, who include the Bafokeng, and hence the Royal Bafokeng Nation. Thus, the crocodile is an element in the RBN's flag. In the flag, the crocodile is moving towards water, which the Bafokeng people believe to be a sign of contentment. The crocodile is depicted by other Basotho-Batswana groups with its mouth open, whereas the Bafokeng have always depicted their crocodile with its mouth shut.

I was astounded as my young tour guide explained the character traits of the tribes with those that belong to the crocodile with an open mouth versus the closed mouth. Contentment can paint and taint the whole picture. A well-fed crocodile is content; it does not present danger as he heads for the water, yet it commands respect by its nature. However, the crocodile with an open mouth will shred anyone in its path-destruction and devastation. It is how the tribe's culture and tone are created. This also shines the light on the rest of humanity, and you will trace underlying behaviour patterns or conditioning that drives a person. Preconditioning will always remain a solemn blight on human nature. Unless you make the journey to explore this, any phobia shackled to it takes a great resonance-refrain from being confined to utopian dreamers. Step outside the square to zoom in.

I had to glean my contentment. I acquired strategic skills to work in an unfair world. I learned to love relentlessly after having my heart shredded. I had to assemble new ways to laugh. I had to garner all the courage to forgive. I had to deliberately collect time for recreation. I gathered time to pray. And I had to develop the techniques to hustle. I obtained newfound appeal, I taught myself to master the critical juncture, and I assembled time to introspect and become self-aware. I absorbed how to sink or swim with the kiss of Judas and fight for the guiding light to unravel my path. I stood tall in resolve with my insufficiencies and advantages – I dived in to close the gap. I decided to cry when I needed to. I studied the drive behind love and hate. Contentment is most definitely about a skillset and conscious choice: focus, perspective, deliberation, resolution, expectation, flexibility, restraint, evaluation, and selection. It is not insignificant but relative and a telling sign when we accept the outcome for a situation. An outcome that we engineered actively or passively. We find contentment in what we say yes and no to. We persevere, transform, or compromise – that art of living, a.k.a. contentment.

We advocate for a life disconnected from replications but strong on serving up pleasure. Life is about balance, and the equation will never be balanced when you do NOT understand how sowing and reaping affects your life. You can only get out what you put in. Paul knew the full range of human experience, and he says in the Bible, *"In every circumstance, I have learned to be content."* Contentment is a grace learned over time. The implication of the word **'learned'** is that it was not always like this for Paul. He grew in contentment over time. And so, begins the journey for every person. You control your destination and how fast you reach it. Contentment can be an elusive pursuit. We chase after what we consider will make us happy, only to discover that the void prevails. In the scripture, as mentioned earlier, Paul talks about what I have **learned to be content**. From this, we glean that contentment is not something that's gifted to us by default, but rather, we must learn it.

Learning to be content in every season of life involves cultivating a mindset of gratitude and acceptance. It starts with recognising the blessings we have, no matter how small, and shifting our focus from what we lack to what we possess. Practising mindfulness helps us stay present, allowing us to appreciate each moment fully. Additionally, setting realistic expectations and embracing change as part of life's journey can foster resilience. Surrounding ourselves with supportive relationships and engaging in reflective practices, such as journaling or prayer, can further deepen our sense of peace. Ultimately, contentment is a skill that requires intentional effort and a willingness to grow.

One of my extracurricular activities includes fine dining. It is a small reward for my hard work. I love travelling and exploring new food and cultures. No matter how many stamps I have in my passport, I never feel content. I have not yet reached a place where *"this is done and dusted."* The culinary exquisite luxuriate can put a strain on the offshore bank account. Yet I understand that this is my bottomless cup. It is where my pleasure thrives. I discovered that *"how"* is never as important as *"why"* in my contentment equation. When you discover the simple pleasures of life, hold onto it and improve the formula. I still salute every morning with a heart that still has remnants of ache, but I choose to marshal my way through it. I have resolved to create something alluring each day. I quest for nothing more than giving rather than taking; this is where I find my joy. Scripture in Matthew 20:28 reflects, *"Just as the Son of man did not come to be served, but to serve."* Denotes that Jesus came to earth, and He was content to serve. He found His passion, a.k.a. contentment.

Your mind is a garden; your thoughts are the seeds. You can grow flowers, or you can grow weeds. Only you can grasp the gist of your life, how you sow, and what you reap. A smile can open the heart faster than a key can open the door. Smiles are spontaneous; don't hoard them. Revitalise your world and attain your true contentment. *"You will face many defeats in life, but never let yourself be defeated."* – Maya Angelou. Refrain from derailing your life and being trapped in the mindset that constantly wonders what may go wrong and begin to get excited about what could go right. Love yourself unconditionally and understand what is suitable for you; refuse to tolerate, decline to accommodate mediocrity, reject anything and anyone that robs your peace, and rebuff the attitude of chaos. No one is going to love you precisely like you envisage. No one is ever going to unravel your mind and pick up a flower from the field and hand it to you exactly when you need it. My life experience has taught me that amidst the despair, I was invisible; my pain was not broadcast on my sleeve, and even those who knew of my battles cared not to lighten the load. There is never a knight in shining armour. I had to resort to seeking my contentment in every circumstance.

During my vacation to Fiji Island, I discovered Garden Island of Fiji, situated in the heart of the International Date Line. It is located on the 180th meridian from the royal observatory. In essence, this means half the island is today, and the other half is still stuck in yesterday. A dilemma above most salary grades. We all develop mechanisms to live favourably with the set circumstances. We all find ways, even in the most bizarre conditions. According to locals, New Year's in Taveuni was once a huge celebration. Locals would throw two parties, celebrating the new year on both sides of the calendar. Shops on Taveuni once happily claimed that they were the first to open in the world.

Despite the dateline that splits Taveuni and the islands east of Taveuni, Fiji opted to nudge its borders to fit the entire country within one time zone. All the citizens found contentment with this. Have you progressed enough to grasp your contentment? Are you entertained by the label that you categorised yourself with as a mature person but still wear fatigue, unenthusiasm, and concern, like foundation on your face?

What purports to measure CONTENTMENT? Do you have a proverbial checklist? Even when you reach the top of your game, do you still thirst for more? Kobe Bryant was at the top of his game, raking it in. At his time of death, Kobe Bryant's net worth was estimated to be $600 million. He was a former American professional basketball player and entrepreneur. He played his entire 20-year career in the NBA with the Los Angeles Lakers. Bryant was considered to be one of the best NBA players of all time, won multiple awards and trophies during his career, and was also one of the wealthiest athletes of all time. It came as an enormous shock to the world when he was pronounced dead after a tragic helicopter crash on the way to his daughter's basketball game. His daughter and several others were also killed. It's common to know that successful parents groom their kids to follow in their footsteps or perhaps something. Crystalline clarity sometimes goes on vacation and stays on vacation. The taste of success drives for even more fame, fortune, and wealth.

Seemingly gregarious life and lifestyle that can be maintained with the present acquired wealth, but human nature strives for more. Insatiably curious about the future, this dad was grooming his daughter to walk in his footsteps, perhaps. Catching a helicopter to a basketball game with your child confirms priorities, a correlation to where we find contentment, possibly not staying home and playing with Barbie and her friends. This dad had a vision for his daughter and his family. We all have our visions and goals for life. We savour the privilege of the anchored seat when we attain our dreams, yet satisfaction still eludes us. Insisting on putting on a great mood, we then begin to chase a new dream. Contentment begins when you glide to where the pluck is to soothe your heart.

Many souls are exhausted with murmurings, lives perishing away with grumbles and indulgence that creates a morbid amusement but no genuine chi in their vitality. Where is the stimulant for the fragrant, serene stances of contentment? It is akin to utopia; however, we do not have this because the blueprint of our mind is chaotic. We have become accustomed to being on the wheel like hamsters. Going nowhere but getting exhausted. We are deficient in the feeling of contentment under all circumstances. Most free spirits will condone anything for a portion of peace. Yet so rarely does society pray and ask God: Guard me from purposeless dreads, predicaments of the world, and the allurements of the heart. Some people have created a habit to distract themselves from their thoughts and refuse to seek their fruit that will make them happy. Ardently interested in themselves but not strategic with long-term sustained satisfaction.

What variety of blind recreations have you imprisoned? Are you linked in chains with short-term delight? Who have you bound in crude patterns? When you act as the contract mandates, and you are cheated, it is difficult to trace the presence of contentment. *Laban first appears in the Bible in Genesis 24:29-60 as the grown spokesman for his father Bethuel's house; he was impressed by the gold jewellery given to his sister on behalf of Isaac and played a key part in arranging their marriage. Twenty years later, Laban's nephew Jacob was born to Isaac and Rebekah. When grown, Jacob comes to work for Laban. Laban promised his younger daughter Rachel to Jacob in return for seven years of service, only to trick him into marrying his elder daughter Leah instead. Jacob then served another seven years in exchange for the right to marry his choice, Rachel, as well.*

Jacob loved Rachel, and he was content to work another seven years for the love of his life. He refrained from ranting and raving about the contract not being fulfilled as stipulated. Contracts are complicated, and working with family is difficult – choose your difficulty. Jacob understood the art of contentment. Marriage is challenging, and divorce is challenging, pick your challenge. Integrity is demanding, and insincerity is demanding – select your demands. You may not always see the results of your actions, but every ounce of positive energy will contribute towards your storehouse of contentment. You are not required to roam in barren quests after contentment as if it is a wild beast that you chase. Be still and trace the contours of your own heart. Your maker will reveal Himself to you and the path that He directs. Contentment is not attained like a university qualification and boasted on your LinkedIn profile. It is where the rubber hits the road – the character you have created from day one and the joys YOU entrapped therein.

Successively, distrust debilitates one's potential personally and professionally. It also cheats people of contentment, progress, and experiencing relational genuineness. The most operational journey to creating phenomenal satisfaction begins with association to your very primal navigating method called intuition. Awareness combined with proficient expertise is an influence of invention that forms the bedrock for contentment. When you discover your potent insight and apply intuitive decision-making practices in any given circumstance personally and professionally, you will forever reap contentment. It will allow you to regulate and dominate your life terms and your framework of contentment. It is a welcome reprieve to be the master of your life even when you are not accustomed to a good mood. That's not a promise but rather a purpose. Proving yourself in a local endeavour will set you up for a more fantastic future. Rekindle the fear of your darkest days and march on.

It is modelled so well to us by the life of David Attenborough. *"He spent his childhood collecting fossils, stones, and natural specimens. Attenborough was educated at Wyggeston Grammar School for Boys in Leicester. He won a scholarship to Clare College, Cambridge, in 1945 to study geology and zoology and obtained a degree in natural sciences. Attenborough was a senior manager at the BBC, having served as controller of BBC Two and director of programming for BBC Television in the 1960s and 1970s. First becoming prominent as host of Zoo Quest in 1954, his filmography as writer, presenter, and narrator has spanned eight decades; it includes Natural World, Wildlife on One, the Planet Earth franchise, The Blue Planet, and its sequel. He is the only person to have won BAFTA Awards in black and white, colour, high definition, 3D, and 4K resolutions."*

Over his life, he has collected dozens of honorary degrees and awards, including three Emmy Awards for Outstanding Narration. He is the most travelled person in the world. While Attenborough's earlier work focused more on the wonders of the natural world, his later work has been more vocal in support of environmental causes. He has advocated for restoring planetary biodiversity, limiting population growth, switching to renewable energy, mitigating climate change, reducing meat consumption, and setting aside more areas for natural preservation. On his broadcasting and passion for nature, NPR stated he *"roamed the globe and shared his discoveries and enthusiasms with his patented semi-whisper way of narrating."* He is widely considered a national treasure in the UK, although he does not like the term.

Attenborough had a pacemaker fitted in June 2013 and a double knee replacement in 2015. In September 2013, he commented: *"If I was earning my money by hewing coal, I would be very glad indeed to stop. But I'm not. I'm swanning around the world looking at the most fabulously interesting things. Such good fortune."* I reckon this is the patent voice of contentment. David found his passion, and within, he found his contentment by using every possible avenue to align with his purpose and vision. Enthusiasm does not have an expiration date – labour makes it harder to create a culture of fulfilment.

Every day is a new day to try and fail rather than fail to try. The story is not over when you are perched precariously, struggle with unvarnished attempts, chase your tail in a rudimentary fashion, lose your laser focus, and become heavily error-prone and baffled by science. David retorted to a content life by meandering his passion. Unearth yours.

"The greatest happiness of life is the conviction that we are loved – loved for ourselves, or rather, love in spite of ourselves." – Victor Hugo.

How satisfied are you with...

- Are you content with what you have currently acquired, or do you still yearn for more?

- Forgiving yourself for the choices you made when you did not know you had better options. Focus on growing and moving on toward your contentment.

- Look back at the terrain of your life and map out your contentment diary. How content are you with how life has turned out? If you are unhappy, what will lead you to contentment?

Superficial Satisfaction

The lack of contentment that grades society is redirected in many modes. It is evident in our astronomical rate of consumer debt. We are most definitely not content to live within our means, so we splash out on a quest into debt to live just a tad better. Our discontent is reflected in our excessive rate of movement. Statistics reveal that people seldom stay at the same address for more than five years. Our behaviour sets in motion a series of decisions that culminate in our level of satisfaction. In addition, discontentment rears its head in our exorbitant divorce rate. Pleasure eludes our marriages, so we upgrade our companions for the latest versions. Our deficiency of contentment is seen in the bellowing for our entitlements. We are prosecuting one another at a flabbergasting frequency. All ruin eventually leads to a vacuum; consistently avoid building an abyss. Instead, live with the purpose of clarifying what, when, who, why, and how your contentment tank is powered. The lust for external goods does not last forever; do not be trumped by false expectations.

Liberty, tolerance, relief, resilience, and self-love all contribute to our contentment. A practise consisting of mere superficial thrills or carnal desire may fire your neurotransmitters to the moon and back; however, it is a relatively short-lived pleasure. Intense pleasure is typically associated with optimal functioning. We are harnessing capabilities and outlooks over a sustained period in an enriching experience. Fragments of profound gratification are the ability to overcome complications and make some advancement. Happiness cannot be attained by merely repeating a superficial, pleasant experience. Contentment is not an isolated attainment but rather a constant, dynamic strategy. We encounter an array of emotions daily, and our happiness should not directly correlate with the emotions of the day, week, or hour. Granted that the state of happiness is evolving, we need to reach a point where our emotions do not drive us. Resolve to find your equilibrium despite your emotional levels.

Logically, happiness as a sentiment consists of the acute emotions of joy, so a succession of specific positive experiences will increase our long-term happiness. No – you will not feel happier if you buy that dress, handbag, or whatever in the long term. When your life is sprinkled with something more fulfilling, like a sweet fellowship with a good friend, you will find it more rewarding. There is no genie or virtual assistant to bring you to a place of contentment. The tenacity to empower and discover genuine contentment lives within yourself. Like happiness, deep love also does not consist mainly of limited enchanted moments; instead, we all need a composed regimen of simple gratifications with our cherished others. Profound love is not a magic tonic. It is found in mundane everyday life – the come-hell or high-water moments, and you still trudge together with all the battle scars.

While the road to profound happiness and love involves many superficial joys, the presence of such delights does not ensure that these profound experiences will necessarily emerge unless you craft it, implement it, and measure it in your life. Live with your eyes and heart open to what takes you on the road to rediscovery and, eventually contentment. Nothing comes easy. Not contentment. Not bliss. Not love. Not the right husband. Not the precise career. Not the spot-on friends. Not success or even a perceptive family. Everyone must peel away superficial satisfaction by the bucketload to eventually find refinement, poise, and contentment as priceless jewellery. We have fashioned a life of misfortunes by indulging in a battle towards some unknown destination. We ought to toil on our destructive attitudes and actions to detoxify our souls. Utopia says the goal of life is to reach a coveted state of happiness. What's your reality? My truth is to find peace so calm that I can sleep in the storm. In the Bible, it depicts that Jesus was asleep on a cushion in the stern, and the disciples woke him and asked, *"Teacher, don't you care if we drown?"* The Gospel of Mark then states that He woke up and rebuked the wind, and said to the sea, *"Peace! Be still!"* Then the wind ceased, and there was a dead calm.

When you live in a place knowing the authority you have within, you exercise dominion over the situation. No person, situation, or status will guarantee you contentment. Enhance your perception and build constructively to radiate beauty from within. When you learn to acknowledge, own, and accept your inner contribution, then your choice of experiencing peace, love, contentment, and happiness becomes more than evident and diffuses its beauty from all junctions of your life. Disappointment is an inevitable part of life. If you never fail, you are probably reaching for low-hanging fruit. When you learn to confront disappointment and glean from its education, you will find a road to contentment that makes life easier to traverse.

It is an invitation to seek contentment.

Not with the kind of superficial desire that is based on what your bank balance is, what you have prospered at, what others contemplate of you, or whether you were able to hold it together and appear unified today. It is a summons to get reflective, intense, insightful, and contemplative with yourself. The self-analysis that is so robust that it makes you awkward in its power – and yet you KNOW you require it. Dig deep to unleash the constraints and evaluations on:

- The ones that profess to love you but paint a different story with their actions
- Your disillusionments
- External facades
- The perception that others have of you
- Desire to please
- Forgiving those that you trusted
- The list of your acquisitions

- Social media persona
- Some profess to be friends but refuse to support you online, closed-door pretence

Get detached from these superficial things in life.

Craft the contentment that you don't have to strive for, aspire to, or slave over, but rest in the arms of what you reap here NOW. It is the serenity that shreds all the barriers and discloses who you TRULY are. The gratification that leaves you so unblemished on what legacy you desire to leave behind:

- The contentment that compels you
- The gratification that humbles you
- The pleasure that cures you
- An ease that reconciles you
- A gladness that repairs you
- A thirst that nurtures you
- A satisfaction that transforms you
- A fulfilment that ignites you
- An indulgent that strengthens you

It is the essential satisfaction: contentment uninhibited by obligations, judgments, reproaches, unrealistic expectations, comparisons, anxiety, or distress. Cease the struggle, untraditionally release whatever is weighing on your lovely soul, and enter a place of liberation. Life, after all, is not so tranquil. But as George Bernard Shaw said, *"Life is not meant to be easy, my child; but take courage – it can be delightful."* It is a guarantee that you will have days where you feel like you are on top of the mountain and days where you feel like you have hit rock bottom. Escalating from the fragments requires going through the infernos. The deterioration is the beautiful process towards contentment. The courage it takes to leave behind what's not for you anymore is the same audacity that will help you find your way toward contentment. You will weed out dissatisfaction like you are on autopilot. The stance is to replace why this is happening to you with what this is trying to impart to you, then you can watch the narrative change.

As a rational creature, do you understand your eternal perspective and the profits of this life? Have you won the tug-of-war with your moral-psychological mechanisms? Are you in the game of converting something to feel a level of satisfaction? Fleeting amusement, indulgence, prosperity, privilege, and the whole gamut of fabrications that measure human joy. Have you seriously pondered the rebound effects with a genuine gap analysis to help fill the void and stimulate more empirical attainment to find what turns on your contentment? To this end, dig deep and ask yourself the basic what, why, who, where, and how questions. Based on this conceptualisation and integrating facts, invite your moral licence to run this race and win. This endeavour will outline promising directions for your future.

Have you ever felt like your emotions are fake in public or private? Do you struggle to legitimise your emotions? Do you feel good or bad about yourself? Do you love or hate your personality? Has trauma transformed you into an emotionless person? In psychological terminology, this is classified as depersonalisation, and it is a dangerous territory to live in. Have you discovered what your moral duty is? What makes life tolerable for you? Is your contentment embroiled in blandishment and anticipation? Some say you cannot find happiness when you are looking for it; others say happiness does not equate to contentment. Whatever your parameters are, contentment is not based on an external situation or factors that you can manipulate. Nothing may fill the hollowness of a soul. Has anyone tagged you as a shallow person? *Shallow* is an offence; *deep* is an accolade. *Shallow* is synonymous with *greedy, unsuccessful, self-centred, self-indulgence, single-minded, unreserved,* and *narcissistic.*

Deep-natured people are instinctively considered knowledgeable, compassionate, ingenious, appealing, morally robust, and perceptive. At large, most people are a combination of both; I guess it depends on which side of the bed you get up from or which one you starve or feed. You can control both the positive and the negative. Perhaps you are swimming in a lake that's drowning you and your insecurities about being superficial. If the task is too difficult for you to realign from superficial to satisfied, then you are denying yourself true contentment. When you prefer to purely glide on the surface, then you block life-changing insights from lived experiences. Who crafts your character? You, your parents, your spouse, God, your dog? Oh, the revelation has dawned on you; now get cracking. Following much action that oscillates uncultivated behaviours; yes, indeed, it may be tough to trudge a new path but persevere.

Sprout enthusiasm for new and superior things. Icarus, from Greek mythology, is a classic example of hubris. Icarus flew too close to the sun, and his wings melted, and he fell to earth. In layman's terms, hubris is excessive pride or self-confidence. You must break up with hubris if you want to marinate in the flavours of contentment. People who do not decide their futures choose their daily practices, and their norms dictate their futures. The dehumanising dimensions of this era have created a culture that has imprisoned people in apprehension, melancholy, and anguish, which is the opposite end of the spectrum from contentment. With foresight, understanding, and enlightenment, you can find the path to satisfaction on any chaotic road. Search for the principle that prescribes your contentment.

Stigmatising mistakes ruins innovation and intellectual risk ventures. Vincent Willem Van Gogh was a Dutch post-impressionist painter who posthumously became one of the most famous and influential figures in Western art history. Not commercially successful, he struggled with severe depression and poverty, eventually leading to his suicide at age 37. Van Gogh suffered from psychotic episodes and delusions, and though worried about his mental stability, he often neglected his physical health, did not eat properly, and drank heavily. His friendship with Gauguin ended after a confrontation with a razor when, in a rage, he severed part of his left ear. He spent time in psychiatric hospitals. His depression persisted, and on July 27, 1890, Van Gogh is believed to have shot himself in the chest with a revolver, dying from his injuries two days later. Van Gogh was commercially unsuccessful during his lifetime, and he was considered a madman and a failure. As he only became famous after his suicide, he came to be seen as a misunderstood genius in the public imagination. Today, Van Gogh's works are among the world's most expensive paintings to have ever sold, and his legacy is honoured by a museum in his name, the Van Gogh Museum in Amsterdam, which holds the world's most extensive collection of his paintings and drawings.

Are you a despondent brilliance? Is your personality inherent? Instead of focusing on the negative, concentrate on the positive. Open yourself up to new escarpments, hypotheses, knowledge, rational curiosity, and emotional fortitude. Retain your energy for greater matters. As we read earlier, Paul from the Bible modelled to us that contentment is not based upon circumstances. Mettle to seek your contentment in every situation that life hurls. Contentment comes from within and tolerates any spectrum of circumstances to come out trump. It does not denote ignoring reality and pretending that problems don't exist. It means dealing with the situation until you find a remedy that brings harmony. When you refuse to deal with the root cause of the issues, then you invite frustration, and then you begin to flirt with bitterness.

Certain people debate that happiness is not continually achievable because, at times, there is going to be disagreement and misery. Hit pause on the load of trepidation. Chocolate is delectable; it transports most of us to a happier place. Yet, we do not consume it constantly. We maintain a balanced diet for a valid reason. We still live content lives without consuming chocolate all day, every day. We are satisfied with the absence of chocolate. Self-awareness, synchronisation, caution, and appreciation produce a content person and a wholesome mind. The origins of an unsettled mind and a discontent person can be found in dishonesty and a complicated and ungrateful life. Symptoms are anxiety, fear, dread, and distress, with many more potentially damaging manifestations. Frequently, we find a solution to treat the symptoms rather than the root cause.

In 2022, I visited Tasmania, Australia. On my bucket list was the option to explore Port Arthur and enjoy a personalised tour. Port Arthur offers a glug of history; it boasts a landscape of natural beauty, scenic ruins, and sandstone-restored buildings. I endeavoured to make the most of my day-sunscreen, hat, and sunglasses whacked on and ready to rumble. As we parked our car in the inclined car park and walked down to the historic site, we saw a breathtaking view. I watched the sun nestle onto the lush green escarpment, and I had a sense of peace and calm of the serenity that opened to captivate my audience. My visual was punctuated when my husband broke the silence to reveal that this is the site of a massacre. My insatiable inquisitiveness lurked.

The mass shooting occurred on April 28, 1996, at Port Arthur, a tourist town in the Australian state of Tasmania. The perpetrator, Martin Bryant, killed 35 people and wounded 23 others, the worst massacre in modern Australian history. The attack led to fundamental changes in Australia's gun laws. Bryant pleaded guilty to the killings and received 35 life sentences without parole; his motives have been subject to debate. In 1992, Martin Bryant, then 25, was bequeathed about $570,000 in property and assets by a friend, Helen Harvey, who left her estate to him following her death in a car crash. He used part of this money to go on many trips around the world from 1993 onwards. Bryant's father had tried to purchase a bed and breakfast property called Seascape, but Noelene (also known as Sally) and David Martin bought this property before his father could ready his finances, much to the disappointment of Bryant's father, who often complained to his son of the *"double-dealing"* the Martins had done to secure the purchase. Bryant's father offered to buy another property from the Martins at Palmers Lookout Road, but they declined the offer. Bryant apparently believed the Martins had deliberately bought the property to hurt his family and believed this event to be responsible for the depression that led to his father's 1993 suicide. Bryant later described the Martins as *"very mean people"* and *"the worst people in my life."*

In late 1995, Bryant became suicidal after deciding he had enough. He stated, *"I just felt more people were against me. When I tried to be friendly towards them, they just walked away."* Although he had previously been little more than a social drinker, his alcohol consumption increased and, although he had not consumed any alcohol on the day of the massacre, had significantly escalated in the six months prior. According to Bryant, he thought the plan for Port Arthur might have first occurred to him four to twelve weeks before the event. After I discovered all this profound history, my brave spirit was disillusioned. I still remember more than I expected, and I forgot less than I hoped to.

This tragic history confirms that money does not equate to happiness, which automatically correlates to contentment. This thread is complex, just like life itself. The genealogy modelled defeat; this is a vortex that's so much could have, should have, and would have happened. Bryant was seeking approval and acceptance from a mob that did not value him. Sadly, he placed his value on external factors that he could not persuade. You will never find contentment if you pursue it from others. You don't have to ask the whole world if you should quit your job, move houses, have a baby, or marry. It denotes that you don't know for yourself what the correct answer is, and you cannot tell how to attain your contentment; you are hoping others will lead you to it. You will never find contentment in navigating with other people's answers. It's best to see what your heart needs and where you need to travel to feel content.

I attended a charity ball in Sydney, Australia, for men's mentoring. The keynote speaker was a Navy officer elaborating on the dangers of suicide among men. The lady sitting to my right was a mum, and we exchanged banter. She proceeded to communicate about the recent suicide in her children's school and commented on how social media was driving teenagers to disillusionment and suicide. No doubt the issue is real and out of hand. The Port Arthur massacre occurred before social media stole the narrative. While there is an element of truth to any given situation, there is also an underlying current that is not always visible. I am an international bestselling author, and social media serves as a platform to broadcast my core message. Every day, people tell me how they hate social media and how I should liaise with them directly and send them pictures personally. I'm also acutely aware of how many people are following me but refuse to acknowledge it with a like or a comment. It's a telling sign when I post a video, and there's 2000 views but 150 likes. Rest assured; I understand the undercurrent at play. My confidence, character, brand, and contentment are not entangled in external factors or social media. It takes a balanced individual to sift out the wheat from the chaff.

Defeat, indeed, but not murder – satisfaction will alert you if you resort to the latter. Have faith in the light you carry, no matter how difficult the circumstances are. Create decisions that bring big enough hope in times of desolation. Understand that the more wrinkles mock you in the mirror when you dwell on the past, superficial elements, or you place your joy in someone else's hands. Contentment takes its inspiration from the chambers of your heart. The glossary of contentment is found in the characteristics of enduring inner peace, independent of external factors; no matter what contrived curveball comes hurling your way, you can craft a conquering attitude. You may be rattled but never distraught in the face of adversity. You will dance even if it rains. Be defiant!

This harks back to the era of characters that were built to stand the test of time and have a splendid time living it. To live a rewarding life, you must understand the character you bring to the theatre of life. While some circumstances are thrust up upon you, only you define the storyline of your truths.

You can live with such certainty and absolute honesty that one day; you can declare you did not know what contentment was until you knew what contentment was not. In essence, you fashion a sense of tranquillity, delight, and contentment even when your circumstance is not totally desirable. You need to stir up acumen in bucket loads to discern your focal point of both good and bad themes in your life and how you resolve to find the balm to your soul. Disclaimer: the easy way out will never lead you to contentment. Even in adversity, you will realise that the moment is the moment, and internally, you still are who you are. Tomorrow or next week, the moment and your emotions will feel different. Refrain from making choices that will trap you for life based on what you are feeling for a fleeting moment.

Contentment will chase you down when you have grasped how to enjoy what remains when you are standing in the ruins. *"It's your attitude, not your aptitude, that determines your altitude."* – Zig Ziglar. Truth be told, failure is a detour, not a dead-end street. When you are wounded, dig deep to find what energises you. Don't dwell on injury, persecution, and betrayal; it will lead you to a dark place. Life is a battlefield; when you are wounded, you don't give up. Prepare to learn from the battle and win the war. I found my sure foot of contentment in the depths of despair when I realised, I didn't have the strength within me to assert with the vicissitudes of life. I reached out to God for help, and He directed my soul to find peace in this scripture from Habakkuk 3: 17-19.

"Though the fig tree does not bud and there are no grapes on the vines, though the olive crop fails, and the fields produce no food, though there are no sheep in the pen and no cattle in the stalls, yet I will rejoice in the Lord, I will be joyful in God, my Saviour. The Sovereign Lord is my strength; He makes my feet like the feet of a deer; He enables me to tread on new places".

Suicide rates around the world present a stark reality: the latest statistics reveal a troubling increase in lives lost, with millions struggling to find meaning and contentment amid overwhelming challenges. This lack of fulfilment can push individuals towards the tragic decision to end their lives, highlighting the urgent need for a deeper understanding of contentment. As we face this global crisis, it becomes clear that fostering resilience and finding a personal blueprint for contentment is essential. By learning to navigate our circumstances – no matter how difficult, we can shift the narrative and provide support for those who feel trapped in despair, ultimately reducing the staggering toll of lost lives.

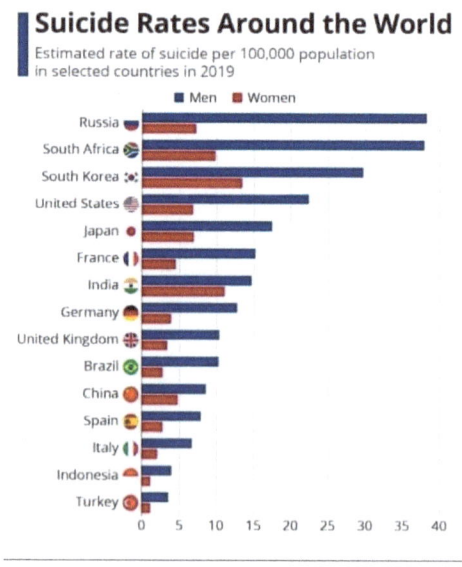

Global Suicide Statistics in 2019

In your quest for contentment, it's vital to embrace a mindset that leaves no stone unturned. The journey often feels daunting, especially when you are grappling with pain, loss, or uncertainty. However, within your struggles lies the potential for growth and fulfilment. Here are some tips to creating contentment:

Acknowledge the Pain
The first step is acknowledging the pain you feel. It's easy to dismiss your emotions or push them aside in the hope that they will disappear. Yet true contentment cannot be built on a foundation of unresolved feelings. By confronting your pain, you begin to understand its roots and how it shapes your perspectives. Journaling, talking to a trusted friend, or seeking professional support can provide the clarity you need to see beyond your immediate struggles.

Cultivate Self-Compassion
Next, you must practice self-compassion. In a world that often encourages comparison and self-criticism, it's crucial to treat yourself with kindness. Allow yourself to feel vulnerable and recognise that everyone faces challenges. Self-compassion creates a safe space for healing, helping you to accept your current situation while nurturing the hope for a better future.

Explore New Perspectives
Leaving no stone unturned involves exploring new perspectives. This can mean challenging ingrained beliefs about what happiness and contentment should look like. Engaging with diverse viewpoints – through books, podcasts, or conversations with people from different backgrounds, can inspire you to redefine your understanding of fulfillment. Sometimes the most profound insights come from unexpected sources.

Set Intentional Goals
As you navigate your pain, setting intentional goals can guide you toward contentment. These goals should be realistic and aligned with your values, allowing you to take small steps forward. Whether it's prioritizing self-care, pursuing a hobby, or nurturing relationships, each action, no matter how minor, contributes to a sense of purpose and achievement. Celebrate these milestones, as they are vital to fostering a positive mindset.

Finding contentment amidst pain is not easy, but by leaving no stone unturned, you can uncover pathways to fulfillment. Acknowledging your pain, practicing self-compassion, exploring new perspectives, setting intentional goals, embracing mindfulness, seeking connection, and committing to growth are all essential steps in this journey. Ultimately, while the road may be challenging, the pursuit of contentment enriches our lives and offers hope even in the darkest times.

How content are you with...

- What kind of *"contentment"* rests in your heart that requires no need for outward incentive?

- What can you accomplish more in the next 24 hours, week, month, and lifetime towards your marvellous contentment plan?

- Zoom in on everything you can perform less in the next 48 hours to suggest your restored state of mind.

- How satisfied are you with your level of gratitude and appreciation for where your life is right now?

Complications to Contentment

Love sometimes equates to contentment, each butterfly creating an emotion, and every wrinkle tells a story. Sometimes, you bleed until it hurts, yet YOU paint on your contentment like a flawless foundation. You may border on contentment with all the unleashed give, take, show, and tell. Respectively, every weight that burdens your soul whispers a mantra: Is this love? Am I truly content? True love will love you completely. Spontaneous yet content – the sort of contentment that glistens cheerfully with ease. Contentment sustains control over any situation and does not permit undisciplined desires and unreserved reactions to unravel confusion now when extreme composure is summoned. Contentment soothes the mood, resulting in acting and speaking prudently.

Our era is categorised by intolerance, lavishness, irritable syndrome, rejection, abandonment, and melancholy. It is almost impossible to glimpse the authentic expression of contentment and its sensations. Contentment does not meander its way back to material possessions or anything superficial. Unravelling contentment is not found in complicated ecosystems. It's found in the simple pleasures of life, and it is found in the complex aspects of life that you cannot control but learn to accept. Contentment is a priority when you want to live a fulfilled life. It would help if you learned how to practice it. How do we learn this? Who has modelled this for you?

During my first visit to the Kruger National Park Reserve in South Africa, I watched a documentary. It left me staring blankly to and fro with the majesty of an ancient pharaoh until the silence was broken in a pose of concentration. A lioness who lost all her pride was alone and depressed until she stumbled upon an impala calf. The calf was orphaned and disillusioned as well. It was astonishing to see how two different species took to each other and found solace, camaraderie, and contentment in each other's company. Baffling, but true. Contentment doesn't have to come in a box that is attached to our birthright or species. This documentary gave me profound revelations. Contentment is where the heart finds rest, peace, love, and acceptance. This odd couple sure did enlighten the populace.

You can purchase a bed, but it does not guarantee sleep. You can bargain and shop for pleasure but not happiness. Contentment is the freedom from wanting more; it is the surrender of strife and the beginning of acceptance. It is finding a console after you are wounded – it is the balm that restores your soul. It is understanding the limitations of being a square peg in a round hole yet living abundantly content with the predicament. Just like the two different species living at Kruger National Park – modelled with no rehearsals. You are living in the moment despite the deficiencies. Contentment opens the door to appreciating both wholesome and ruthless experiences. It is the fine capability of understanding, and some days, you will win, and other days, you will learn a hefty lesson. You take a step every day to either sink or swim – a choice that is either regulated or boundless.

Contentment is not about complacency in the expression of things that ought to be transformed. It is a quest to continually reach your best in every circumstance, not the status quo. Satisfaction is not about accepting the average that is served up, either. It is a relentless pursuit to find greater reassurance, and when you find it, you are finally at rest, and peace prevails. It's going to take significant doses of yielding, fixing, understanding, integrity, and intent. It is best to reach the summit so as not to rumble with your maker. It is reaching a place of comprehension that everything and everyone will disappear at some point – change is the only constant. Nothing is infinite; everything has a shelf life. A splendid vision is unravelled in the tapestry of your dreams. Your supreme dread should not be in failure but in succeeding at things in life that don't matter.

We all have self-aggrandising entitlement to a life of contentment. One of the greatest desires for a woman is to experience the joys of conceiving, living every milestone of gestation, and the simple but complicated pleasure of ushering forth a new life to the world – of being a mother. I endeavour to live by my Christian values; some days I feel it, and other days, it is excruciatingly difficult, but I still persevere. There is a strong consensus in the Christian ecosystem to abstain from premarital sex. Freshly out of a divorce, I headed straight under a rock, and I stayed there for a decade. I had no premeditated plan – just healing from my substantial wounds each day. I deliberated to find myself and where I placed my contentment. Life opened so many doors that I couldn't have imagined for me to walk through. I have captured some of this journey in my #1 bestselling book *Don't Just Fly, SOAR*.

I was finding myself and living my best life, and just like that, a decade progressed. A lady from church bought me a vibrator. I was baffled by this gift. Rest assured; I was content with the lack of extracurricular activity in my life. I had already navigated through living with undiagnosed endometriosis, several failed IVF treatments, numerous miscarriages, and the whole gamut. I yearned for my body and mind to find eternal contentment. I hungered for something that no trust fund could buy. Yes, indeed, I desired to have a baby. But life has its path to which I am not privy. It was challenging, enlightening, and liberating in one profound life to reach a place of acceptance, tearing away the dream and throwing it out the window, watching layers of myself break as I struggled to breathe, while the world continued in default mode. Society has no tolerance for pain. I had to teach myself to become a life valedictorian and drive the steep road to contentment myself.

Hanging onto my attitude as if it is a love affair is no easy task. Tourists see the world; however, the wounded experience it. I had to learn to smile and live with the pain of watching my dream die. Eventually, I reached the road to contentment. I travelled the world, I lived with no abandonments, I invested in myself, I bought books, I attended numerous conferences, and I empowered myself. I enabled myself, and I innovated myself, and therein, I restored my mojo. The spring of life was flowing. Blended in with the colourful colloquialisms of everyday banter, life marched on. Then she won me over with her regal presence – the contentment angels showed up. I accepted my measured nonchalance to motherhood. I found my majesty in the mayhem until another reality sprang into pursuit with a roaring gaggle of incoherent jargon; marauding emotions that could kill.

Women who engage in sexual activity weekly or monthly have a lower risk of entering menopause early relative to those who report having some form of sex less than monthly, according to a new UCL study. The researchers observed that women who reported engaging in a weekly sexual activity were 28% less likely to have experienced menopause at any given age than women who engaged in sexual activity less than monthly. The research, published in *Royal Society Open Science*, is based on data from the USA's Study of Women's Health Across the Nation (SWAN). It's the largest, most diverse, and most representative longitudinal cohort study available to research aspects of the menopause transition.

The first author of the study, PhD candidate Megan Arnot, said: *"The findings of our study suggest that if a woman is not having sex, and there is no chance of pregnancy, then the body 'chooses' not to invest in ovulation, as it would be pointless. There may be a biological energetic trade-off between investing energy into ovulation and investing elsewhere, such as keeping active by looking after grandchildren. The idea that women cease fertility in order to invest more time in their family is known as the Grandmother Hypothesis, which predicts that menopause originally evolved in humans to reduce reproductive conflict between different generations of females and allow women to increase their inclusive fitness through investing in their grandchildren."*

During ovulation, the woman's immune function is impaired, making the body more susceptible to disease. Given a pregnancy is unlikely due to a lack of sexual activity, it would not be beneficial to allocate energy to a costly process, especially if there is the option to invest resources into existing kin. The research is based on data collected from 2,936 women recruited as the baseline cohort for the SWAN study in 1996/1997.

Life throws us reasons we cannot fight or flee. I was in my early 40s when I impolitely discovered my body was synthesising to a lifestyle that took me right to the home of menopause. Magnanimity is never drizzled on all humans equally; contentment is not just bottling up all that life hurls your way. Contentment is a daily habit that is applied in every circumstance. Angst, hindrance, and shattered dreams are not neutral behaviours. It is in times like these that our natural impulses take us so far away from the pillars of contentment. I had to look away from my predicament to close that loop for my heart's joy. I had not met my husband, Dave, at this stage, yet my biological clock had expired. I had to keep my attention focused inside – to heal from within. I was under stimulated in certain facets of my anatomy yet pleasantly thriving. Love eventually found me. Yet menopause rocketed into my life with contention; however, I chose not to dwell there.

Many quandaries come our way to becloud and destabilise us. These are entanglements that teach us how to retain a sweet attitude in every circumstance. No matter what card is handed out to you, you can authentically be steadfast, composed, and steer through any commotion. *"Both optimists and pessimists contribute to society. The optimist invents the aeroplane, the pessimist the parachute."* – George Bernard Shaw. If your outlook in life is not just to fly but to soar, then you need to realise you have to be an optimist to achieve this. Life is a paradox of favours and setbacks; only you can decide if your heart is empty or full. Realise that with the progression of time, circumstances ease, and some don't; perhaps you will never overlook the torments that injured you. Always remember the aroma of your future is built on the ruins of today. Staggering in survival mode does not automatically take you to the path where you flourish. Realisation is a conscious decision and a close cousin of contentment. Every choice you make creates a ripple, and it reverberates.

Let your lived experience take you away from what's comfortable and plunge you into a route that brings music to your soul. Awareness and action are two different components. To enhance your life, you need to choose to act consciously; without action, nothing advances. It may mandate you to recess and be deliberately conscious about your reactions and choices, which ultimately leads to your level of contentment. Yes, indeed, the fractured aspects of life can rejuvenate when you permit it. We all create a trajectory for our lives; we either turn left or right, or else we stagnate. When you are in the same dilemma, mindset, and level of contentment next week, the following year, or in 10 years – you created that. When you can focus beyond your remit, then satisfaction finds you. I found my focus in zooming in on helping others rather than dwelling on my limitations, especially on matters that are outside my control.

UNDERSTAND WHAT YOU CAN CONTROL AND WHAT YOU CANNOT. People are more resilient when they focus on things they can do to move forward rather than focusing on the ways that circumstances have conspired to put them in a bind. Focus on actions you can take that will make your situation better. As you engage in those actions, you will find that you feel better about your setbacks. I have personally witnessed both the *Sour Grape Effect* and the *Ostrich Effect* repeatedly in my career, personal life, spiritual realms, entrepreneurial platforms, and networks. It is critical to master this concept for both personal and professional contentment: when you are hiding your head in the sand, the ostrich effect or devaluing sour grapes, affects the task you were unsuccessful at – and therefore neglects an opportunity for exponential development by learning from your blunders and eventually walking the path to contentment.

Does your character prompt you to self-regulate, and does your mind punctuate you too self-correct when necessary? If you answered no, then you have habits and a lifestyle that are plummeting you into demise. Your platitudes, intellect, insight, regulation, and intuition are tools to use and reuse toward contentment. Life has no manual to guide us to the greener pastures of contentment. Instead, it is packaged with trauma, misery, confusion, dysfunction, and unfathomable injustice. Take your pick; you either resent life or live it abundantly. Finding the art to self-regulate amidst harsh reactions will lead you away from denial, ignorance, and unawareness but closer to contentment. You will never be ready for everything in life, but you can live authentically with the knowledge you have. When you soul search, you will find a song that will sing you home and awaken an undisclosed vision that will reconcile your scorched heart.

The initial place you lose the fight is in your rationale. If you think it's perpetual, then indeed, it is unending. If you deliberate there is no hope, then you have lost your optimism. Understand that every hindrance and constraint is temporary. Even when something is set in stone, you can change the narrative. You can still make lemonade from the lemons. Do not allow your life to be governed by your feelings and circumstances. Acknowledge them but release them, and then make decisions from an informed realm. Validate your reality; it will allow you to develop, withstand, and overcome a range of emotions and circumstances. How you master your emotions is what will win you the war.

As a healed person, I wear my trauma like war paint; the scars are still there, but I have left the arena for brighter vistas. You don't have to allow the world or circumstances to change or hem you in, granted that trauma permanently changes us. Normal is a misconception – you can never go back to who you used to be when you have profoundly changed. It is the most significant barrier to retaining contentment when you constantly yearn for who you used to be. The butterfly can never go back to being a caterpillar. Once you have metamorphosized into something new, embrace it. Accept and garnish your new life – disillusionment, learning curves, and all with audacity. Eventually, everything pans out. Permit the emotions and circumstances to change you. Transformation is inevitable; progress is how you handle the change. Sometimes, you win the war, but the war dwells in you, and it becomes a casualty to the fields of contentment. There is dignity in surviving what you thought would shatter you, and there is fulfillment in thriving after that.

There are milestones when you want to close your eyes, catch your breath, and hope life can go back to the way things used to be. I know I did not crumble when life as I knew it evolved. Any path that you are on can lead you to a beautiful destination. It requires your enthusiasm and commitment. Devote yourself to an eye-opener that orders your rationality, unshackles your spirit, stimulates your character, creates hope in your heart, dreams for your future, and ambitions for every season. This is the freeway to contentment. Civilisation is engaged in pursuing the next quick fix and charming itself with superficial quests. I beseech you to become the philosopher, challenger, and illustrator of your garden of contentment. From the ovum to the coffin – this is a finite roadmap. How do you intend to live audaciously? Fulfilment is a choice, not a default option – show up and take one tiny step each day. One day, you are recovering; the next day, you may be wounded again. Both days, you are moving towards contentment.

Optimism may creep in, and then it gets dashed by the vicissitudes of life. Most of our tension on a regular day stem from the way we respond, not the way life is. Modify your response, and all will advance. Live a life that ignites you so that you can revitalise the world. Maybe the saga signified something, or perhaps it was a mere distraction. It doesn't change the fact that you control what it means to you and how it affects you. Let the situation bring you down or inspire you. You are always in the driver's seat. One of the main organs in our body is the heart. The basic functionality of the heart is to carry oxygenated and deoxygenated blood. There is a constant flow. If this configuration has a meltdown, then the results are catastrophic. The same analogy applies to our level of contentment. We need to have a constant flow of what comes in and what goes out. You need to understand the mechanism that you need a method to filter what flows in and out of you. The heart function has a rhythm, and this rhythm cannot be disrupted. The same is applicable for contentment. It is up to you to find your way to pick up all the dilemmas of everyday life and filter them in a fashion that rejuvenates you.

A decent but unscrutinised life will be extreme on compulsion and unlikely to remember the odd enigma, the tongue-in-cheek luck, the ad hoc dilemmas, and the reality of being dust – your end state. Any marketing tools will not brand your dust; seek satisfaction with here and now. Every time you make a choice, you are turning your core into a different version of the person that you were yesterday. Behind you are memories. In front of you are visions, goals, and dreams. Celebrate your achievements with all those who love you. Glean from your setbacks and use the data and history in a meaningful way to fashion something greater. Within you are all the skills and experience needed.

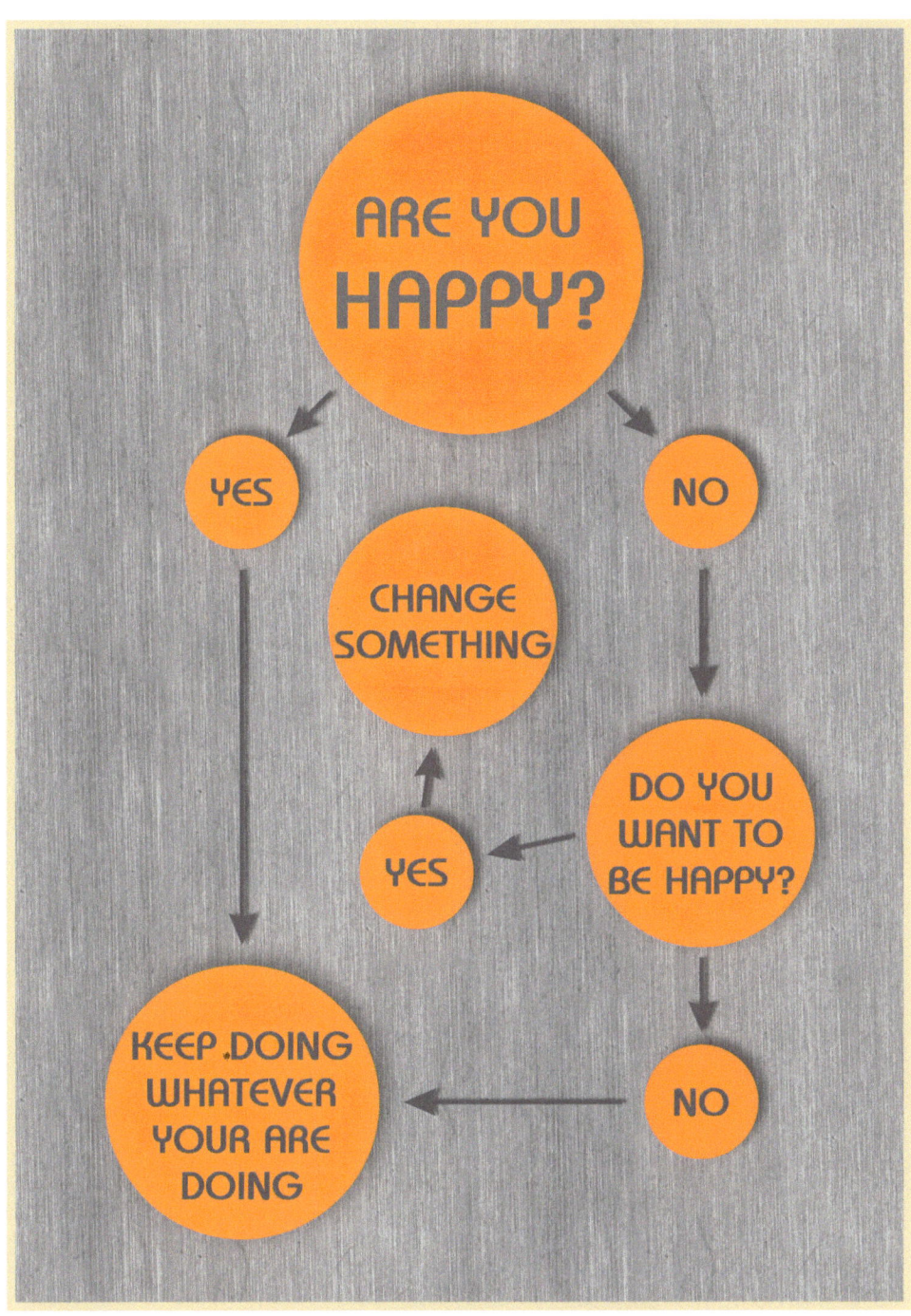

Journey to a Happy or Sad Path

Don't allow commotions to send you down a rabbit hole like Alice. Your peace is precious; safeguard it. Denial and pretence will keep you lost in that burrow. Ride a new wave of experience and reach out and touch contentment. You can choose how you prefer to align yourself; here are some great learning curves from my lived experience.

- Refrain from devoting your life to hunting trivial goals and revering fabricated standards. When this reality dawns on you, then you begin living and are on your way to contentment.

- Understand that you cannot control everything; some outcomes and circumstances are beyond your control. Expect the storm to come and prepare your response.

- It is impossible to please everyone all the time. Prioritise yourself and your nucleus – loved ones.

- There is no tonic to fight health predicaments or the ageing process. Understand the limitations of your body, health, and mind. Choose to live your best every day.

- No one has it all; every person has voids and gaps. Refrain from comparison and judgment. It is where you begin to live an unconventional life that will be your trajectory to contentment.

- Do what's right, especially when no one is watching you. Let it sit well with your soul. Go to bed with peace of mind. This is how the buds of contentment sprout.

- Most want to straighten their curly hair or vice versa. We always seem to want what we do not have. Make peace with your portion. Appreciate your body; it's your vessel that will carry you through life. Create positive ambience.

- Laughter may be the best medication, and authentic happiness may be the boost to life. Go in pursuit of this. And see what finds you.

- All your material assets will decay. The legacy and the way you make people feel are ultimately what lives long after you are gone. Be a storyteller and influence every circle you encounter. Use words if you must – action speaks louder than words.

- Understand that life is not a routine; instead, it is a quest. Live it with no abandonment.

- Do not stockpile the posh crockery and exclusive threads of apparel for a particular day. Baby, you are the specialty. Live like it.

- Grasp that some people will never be fond of you because your breath of life and stimulating principle ruffles their wicked feathers. Make reconciliation with that and march on swiftly.

How content are you with...

- Your level of peace is not to point out someone's true colours. A lack of character will always reveal itself in the end. Are you content with this equation?

- Have you made peace to leave your past behind? It will destroy your future. Love for what today has to offer, not what yesterday has taken away. Contentment is in the beauty of now.

- Recognising and implementing healthy boundaries, especially with family, colleagues, external offenders, and friends, send a clear message that they are allowed to treat you in a certain way that is respectful.

- Does the possibility of learning the art of contentment appeal to you? Or does it bother you? Why?

- Why is it essential to recognise that contentment is not based on circumstances?

Finding your Equilibrium

The brolga, formerly known as the native companion, is a bird in the crane family. It has also been given the name Australian crane, a term coined in 1865 by well-known ornithologist John Gould in his book, *Birds of Australia*. The brolga is a common, gregarious wetland bird species of tropical and south-eastern Australia and New Guinea. It is a tall, upright bird with a small head, long beak, slender neck, and long legs. Its plumage is mainly grey, with black wing tips, and it has an orange-red band on its head. Consider yourself blessed if you ever get to see this bird in the wild. It is a beautiful creature. It gave me so many parallels for the picture of what contentment could look like. A hefty body, yet the tall, skinny legs carry the weight so effortlessly. The natural colour is grey – a colour affiliated with doom and gloom – and yet this bird is a personification of beauty. The orange red on its head depicts confidence on steroids.

So often, we let our circumstances or external limitations drive our level of contentment. The brolga flaunts to me contentment and finesse. When you feel the odds are stacked against you, don't run from your reality. Instead, sit with yourself, and it will force you to confront your deliberations, feelings, dilemmas, and past. Get comfortable with yourself; understand what makes you tick and what sets you apart. Understand the equity you gain by opening your heart and mind while you relax your pace. You don't have to have a solution for everything. Drown out the whispers that tug at your strings of despair. The apex of contentment is when you discover the courage to let go of what you cannot change and open yourself to the vast assortment of probability. It may cost you something substantial. It is a small price to pay for elevation. Use your hindrances to stimulate you rather than frustrate you. You are always in control. There is always an opportunity in every challenging situation.

I went to the foot of the stairs during my routine general practitioner medical appointment in the latter part of 2022. I was at the age and had symptoms that mandated a mammogram. Strike me pink when the results surfaced and toppled the apple cart. A lump was in my left breast. My debut book was taking the world by storm. I was a nominee for an international award. Life was just dandy; I was content. Marinated in love and satisfaction, then the natural progression. Nothing lasts forever. My doctor performed a physical exam and then requested that I have an ultrasound. Ten days lapsed from scheduling the radiology test, having the test, and obtaining the results. Yes, indeed, the longest ten days of my life, waiting to unravel if I have cancer. I had to dig deep to constantly find my equilibrium and focus on the positive rather than drive my conclusions. I was strategically shackled to nothing but purposely connected to everything. **Contentment is a state of the heart unaltered by apparent situations.** Let that sink in. It is not easy to practice;

I had to realign my thoughts, actions, and mood.

I knew contentment like my pulse; this was not the time to let it slip away. Success follows experience. Every season presents an opportunity. Do not let one facet of your life derail you. Stop, exhale, appreciate all the other elements of your life, and then recalibrate. When you allow yourself to reconcile, you are paying courtesy to an influence within. You move away from becoming a victim, and you trudge toward becoming a master of your destiny. You did not go to bed famished. You have Wi-Fi and all the other perks of the developed world. You have terrific apparel to choose from every morning to dress up and show up. You have clean water and fresh air, and your heart is still beating. Be grateful for the little but profound things.

Healing is carrying the torch of unconditional vigour and following your greatest fears into the darkness to find yourself, even when you must wonder why no one is holding your hand in this storm. Restoration arrives when you make peace with the understanding that this is your journey to navigate. Some amazing souls may come to guide you along the way, but please do not bank on it because you will only get hurt in a season when you need nothing but unconditional love. Find gratitude in every experience. Life will create chaos, but chase gratitude, and it will take you to those who love you truly, and you will understand what their presence means to you; therein, you will discover contentment.

Those people who fill your lungs with oxygen will help you fight any battle in life and help you align to contentment no matter what life hurls your way. Expecting people to do what you would do in a situation will lead to disappointment. Accept their reaction to underperform and move on. Focus on what matters: yourself and your welfare. *"The happiness that brings enduring worth to life is not the superficial happiness that is dependent on circumstances. It is the happiness and contentment that fills the soul even during the most distressing circumstances and the most bitter environment. It is the kind of happiness that grins when things go wrong and smiles through the tears. The happiness for which our souls ache is one undisturbed by success or failure, one which will root deeply inside us and give inward relaxation, peace, and contentment, no matter what the surface problems may be. That kind of happiness stands in need of no outward stimulus."* – Billy Graham.

Create a habit of focusing on the contributions of life rather than zooming in on what you have been deprived of. If you want to create positive changes to reach your ladder of contentment, find satisfaction in modest but considerate acts. Smile more, resolve to focus on the pros rather than the cons, marinate in excitement, and discover new things. Purge your life and your mind, express gratitude, refrain from gossiping, and grab the opportunity to do challenging things. Marshal your brave DNA daily. There is an oxymoron about contentment because contentment presents us with the peace of mind and the affirmation required to mend, mature, and advance.

Yet, there seems to be a vacuum. It creates a confidence that unfaithfully keeps you falsely true. Only you can unravel your conviction and the genuine level of contentment you feel. Strip away all the distractions and get real with yourself. Document what you are grateful for. It will help you monitor your development and leave a chronicle for your family and friends to read and be inspired by.

When you are content, you do not require validation – you are not rebuffed by other people's reactions. Contentment is the antidote to endless desiring – yearning for this or that. Authentic contentment unravels to us that accord is not the absence of agony. It begins with acknowledging your limitations as a human, yet you prevail over yourself in every predicament. You make every effort to do the right thing, period. You endeavour to remain positive; you labour to keep going, you embrace what matters, you let go of the futile, you champion the actual course, you endeavour to remain afloat, and you venture to meet each day. Catch the beauty of the sunrise or sunset, and you uncover your poise in the pain. Be thankful for a heart that understands that life will not always be easy. Discern that paths will curve, and lives will distort. People will rise and fall. Be quenched for the soldiers that took on the form of a healing balm for you at your lowest. Obscurity has many tiers and recognise that you may have more questions than answers, but just as the wind changes direction, so can life. Anchor yourself in something that is not constantly fluctuating.

What prompts your honour, advantage, responsibility, and moral obligation today and tomorrow? CURIOUS? Life may shift steeply; however, it's in the modification that you will trace your level of contempt or contentment. You cannot hope for another time or a different life when you are in the vortex of reality. Decide that each moment is substantially adequate – with whatever circumstances. Live like you are fortunate, talk like you are privileged, act like you are advantaged, and when in despair, know undoubtedly that you will conquer. The transformational river of contentment will be your healing and set you free from pomp, affliction, and consequences. Don't underrate how eager people are to continue a facade, step away from the trend and prod for your trophy. Be true to yourself; contentment is the only priceless gem worth chasing. No special sacrament is required – just your authentic heart. The habit of appreciating the present fosters renewed strength even with old pain. You need to wake up to see that every moment is sacred. When the curtain falls, can you say you were content in every circumstance?

Create and curate; do not hold on to heavy things and give you wounds. It's awkward to suffer from chronic neglect of yourself. It takes time to see the fruit of obedience. The fundamental element is understanding what fruit is and what is just a burden. During the season of discovering a lump on my mammography, so many other issues were spinning me in a whirlwind. Two women from South Africa had lives that were stunted in so many facets. They reached out to me for a lifeline to help them create a more fulfilling life. My default mode is to be a giver, so I launched in. They both felt entitled, demanded more, lacked accountability, and showed no trace of integrity. I battled back tears too many times. The buoyancy of my character sustained me, and the charisma I developed from God. To focus on who God is and how far He has brought me; while the actions of mere mortals noticeably affected me, they will not define me.

Alone but pugnacious, some days I rolled out of bed literally with no clue of my future, and these women bit the hands that fed them. My diagnosis was still looming large, yet I had to align myself to feel contentment regardless of the circumstances. I understood the magnitude of choosing my battles and defining where my energy was needed. I established clear boundaries and resolved to remove any additional toxic residue from people who only contracted lip service. A diamond is just a piece of charcoal that controls trauma remarkably well; it has reached the status of contentment when it sits there sparkling. You need to realise when a situation, a friendship, or a business deal is over so you can move forward and use your energy where it truly matters. I had an instant rapport found on GROWTH parallels. Growth is an influential mechanism. It will have you walking around acutely self-aware, eradicating what no longer serves you, responding rather than reacting, and channelling what matters. Evolution includes not constantly eradicating negative people or experiences – understanding the prerequisite to ensure you are not emotionally stunted.

Congratulations to you for reaching the top of your craft. As you muscle your way to the confines of contentment, understand that disappointment says things could be grander. However, perception says that it could be unhealthier. Refrain from mourning about what did not go according to plan. The blueprint of life is that *change is the only constant*. The key is to spend more time appreciating what you have on your plate rather than lamenting about what you do not have. Sometimes, we give selflessly to others, and yet there's no satisfaction. Many covet what you have; they feel entitled to have what you have, and for some strange reason, they get bitter and twisted with you for carving a life that they crave. Remember, this is not your equation. Even though I was approached to help, I helped, and I established my boundaries when I noted what was not leading me down the path of contentment.

Conspiracy will keep you awake all night long; be judicious and do not get caught up in that web.

A perfect connection does not exist. Reliability, respect, transparency, integrity, and open communication are massive gaps in authentic relations. Never make assumptions that the calibre of this association will lead you somewhere wholesome. It will rob you of contentment in so many ways. Be aware, retune, and reflect. When you refuse to redirect this energy, you will wake up one day with barrenness and wonder in a state of mourning, and you will struggle to recognise how you travelled to a path of unhappiness. You cannot create anything that will be authentically beautiful with jealous people. Run for the hills when you detect jealousy. True progress begins when we can work through any challenge rather than attempting to constantly rescue a crisis. It is not your job to rescue a situation. Anything that will flourish requires give and take; when you are doing all the giving, it's a parasitic equation. It is where contentment will leave the building and never return any time soon.

Try not to focus on selective perception but rather on results that are delivered to you on a platter and speak to you louder than words. Even when you do not have all the answers, focus on all the things that you are grateful for. Gratitude is the best remedy. Begin with the extraordinary genius of your existence. Unfluctuating amid agony, misery, and defeat, gratitude helps us to see that our glass of life is usually 90% full. We can be grateful even during the darkest of times when our glass is only 10% full. Reflect on the capacities you have. Reflect on the millions of people who have contributed in some way over your lifetime to sustain you. Reflect on the generous, intelligent abundance of nature that sustains us all. Reflect on the reality of grace and healing. With gratitude, we focus on what we have rather than what we do not have. When we are grateful for the abundance of our lives, we can be happy for others without needing to compare our lives to theirs. Gratitude helps to counter envy and jealousy.

Even incarcerated individuals find reasons to be grateful. Patients who are terminally ill bounce back in reflection and gratitude for what they have rather than do not. Suicides are rising at an astonishing rate. Why? Are we missing a trace or level of contentment? Essential nourishment and well-being do not come from belongings, authority, reputation, or prominence. Reflect on the suicides of incredibly prosperous and talented people to see the truth of this. Mother Teresa modelled this for us on a global platform. Cultivate contentment by letting go of the misconception that affluence, reputation, rank, or prestige equates to happiness. It does make more people jealous, and it awakens the green-eyed monster in every corner that you turn.

Thanks to neuroscience, we understand that our brain is not permanent. It can essentially change – you can foster positive change. Yes, indeed, contentment can be absorbed. Resilience can be learned. Bouncing back can be learned. Hopefulness can be cultured. Forgiveness can be studied, practiced, and conquered. Teaching your brain new ways will never be a walk in the park; it requires effort, introspection, and behavioural changes. It requires practice to sustain lasting change. You can succeed despite your circumstances. The questions are how, where, why, what, who, and when. Only you can define this.

A cynic can learn to become a visionary, and a tense, adverse brain can be taught to become calm and see additional prospects. Life is durable yet fragile. And it is brief; we have finite days. Knowing this enriches your contentment because awareness of your mortality improves the value of this gift of life. It is best that you relish this moment, even if it is not precisely to your taste. The only permanent is change. If we are hurt, take heart that this discomfort will end. When you are pleased, appreciate your delight even more, knowing that our bliss will be fleeting and that more agony, damage, pleasure, harmony, and heartache lie ahead. You cannot pick from a pre-defined prescription and dispense only what you like to yourself. Learn the art of adjustment and the core skill set to mitigate and manage any risk that comes into your life.

Disconnect yourself promptly from constantly annoyed, drama-driven, and self-centred people. It's not your job to transform them. You will find an astonishing life of joy, peace, and contentment when you close the chapter on them. Research indicates even those who have won huge amounts of money in lotteries are not happy. Do not make efforts to think that you can change the trajectory of someone who does not want to put their hand on the plough to change their level of contentment.

When I was in my twenties living in New Zealand, both my ex-husband and I earned above the average wage. Life was relatively comfortable. We were newlyweds and had so many dreams. Finance was paramount. My ex-husband was a qualified panel beater. His employer enforced the *"if you break it, you pay for it"* policy. We had a planned vacation on the horizon. A significant portion of our vacation was unpaid leave. We were excited and counting down to our vacation. It was just another mundane day at work. My ex-husband was repairing a semi-trailer truck. As he attempted to remove the headlight from the vehicle to fix the panel, the headlight broke. As per his employer's policy, he had to replace this headlight. The cost was NZ $600, ouch! He made the purchase, and it was delivered to our home in a box, and he took it to work to get his work completed. He removed the headlight from the box and placed it on the table. It rolled off the table and smashed into a million pieces. I guess you know the policy. Yes, indeed, NZ$1200 in one week, just like that, poof!

How do you discern when to hold someone accountable and when to deploy kindness? How do you discern how to eloquently dance between the two while you reach your yearning fix for contentment? The gloss to ageing beautifully is not to lament what was tarnished but to celebrate what remains – simple, yet so many struggle to implement this. No doubt, I was frustrated; however, I had to hunt for my equilibrium. If I had chosen to remain focused on the issue rather than the future vacation, my contentment tank would have been depleted. The worst thing you can do for yourself is to suppress your emotions. It will eradicate all traces of contentment. Denying your natural response will manifest negative behaviour. Dissect the situation, deal with the emotions and frustrations, and then swiftly move on. External factors like financial circumstances are beyond your control and should not mandate your level of contentment. Socially integrated, healthy, knowledgeable, and resilient individuals know how to navigate setbacks. They have all the markings of a great future, but some shaping is required.

"Progress is impossible without change, and those who cannot change their minds cannot change anything." – George Bernard Shaw. Mental competence does not assure mental skill. No matter how much brain power you have, if you lack the motivation to adjust your mind to circumstances because those curveballs **WILL** come hurling at you, you will spend life chasing your tail. In psychology, two biases spin the wheel. Confirmation bias is seeing what you expect to see. In comparison, desirability bias is seeing what you want to see. These biases do not just thwart you from applying intelligence; they can contort your acumen into a weapon against the truth. In my case, I could have zoomed in on the predicament and allowed it to derail me rather than focusing on my upcoming planned vacation. The first antidote towards contentment is to be enlightened about your biases, especially when you deem you have no bias.

The relationship you have with yourself is the foundation for contentment, regardless of how other people behave in your environment. The average life expectancy is 78 years, while the retirement age is 67. We work for 50 years to perhaps enjoy 11. Start enjoying your life now. No one is guaranteed tomorrow; even if you must spend money on unforeseen circumstances, focus on the journey, not the destination. Never allow confusion to derail you. When situations go south, showing kindness is an expression of who you are and not a motivation to favour the other person. I love the courageous drama that clarifies confusion and reconciles the drift. It does not waste anyone's time but fills the atmosphere with the fragrance of hope where contentment comes to dwell. Commemorate and emulate your life here and now; don't wait for the future to reap serenity – the decision to live in the now heralds satisfaction in all seasons.

The gulf may widen so swiftly that you feel the undercurrent pull off every trace of contentment from your heart. Do not be fooled by psychopathic charm to lash out when the apple cart is toppled in your path. Abstain from acting on destructive yearnings out of love for yourself and others. Endeavour to manage your response. Craft the practice to purposefully introspect and glean at your destructive compulsions. Remind yourself that not acting on destructive emotions enhances your life and builds up your contentment tank. The practice of moderation affords you the opportunity to practice being content even though you are disappointed. Establish this habit of letting your frustration spill onto the canvas of your life. Acknowledge the frustration, but do not feed it; let it dwindle its power to control you. Permit it to weaken and watch how your contentment arises, even amid frustration. It is an exceptionally liberating experience; it releases you to act in profound ways – to demonstrate tenderness.

Remain a soul of mystical allure and break away from the masses that correlate gratification as a source of happiness. Paint a sight to match your dreams. Impeccable! Sensory indulgences or the attainment of chattels. It's fine to enjoy these things, but never let them own you. Appreciate gratification for what it is – simply gratification – and not confuse it with true happiness. Genuine happiness arises through the rehearsal of love, not the gratification of desires. When you are caught off guard and cannot distinguish what truly makes you content, the false elements keep you engrossed, always inducing a whiplash when she glides through the room. Learn to identify this pattern. Wake up from the slumber. Nurturing contentment takes the agony out of misery. Anguish is inescapable, but torment is voluntary. When you catch yourself undergoing dissatisfaction, bitterness, and resentfulness, proactively harness your skills to reach a place of contentment. It will enhance your life and your world in substantial ways. Refrain from complicating life; live and let peace be your guide.

Be happy with what you have while working for what you desire.
Unshackle your loved ones from compulsions to complete you.
Remember, some things need to end for better things to happen again.
Never allow wounded people to extinguish you.

Transform your ashes into art.
Unleash your parents from the dilemma of failure.
Open doors to the best version of yourself
Slam every door shut to toxicity.

Contentment is born when you want to bear great fruits.
You will always reap what you sow, sow wisely.
Release your children from living up to your great expectations.
Learn from every experience, and contentment will chase you down.

GLEAN. PIVOT. SOAR.

In life, we explore the profound impact of acceptance on our overall sense of fulfilment. Often, we equate contentment with external circumstances – our achievements, relationships, or material possessions. However, true contentment arises from an internal shift, allowing us to find peace and satisfaction despite life's inevitable challenges. By unravelling the layers of your desires and expectations, you can embrace the present moment, cultivating resilience and gratitude. This journey invites you to redefine your understanding of happiness, revealing that contentment is not a destination but a state of being you can nurture within yourself, regardless of your external reality.

WHY DO YOU COMPLAIN?

Here are some revelations from the Bible:

Did Moses stay in the river throughout his life? NO

Did Joseph stay in the prison or the pit forever? NO

Did Shadrach, Meshach, and Abednego stay forever in the fire? NO

Did Daniel stay forever in the Lion's den? NO

Was Esther enslaved forever? NO

Did Hannah stay barren forever? NO

Did Abraham stay childless forever? NO

Did Bartimaeus stay blind forever? NO

Did Lazarus stay in the grave forever? NO

Was Jairus' daughter dead forever? NO

Did Jesus stay in the tomb forever? NO

This is a God given confirmation that you will NOT stay where you are forever. Don't let your faith die; don't give up hope. Don't allow the voice of what you are going through to be louder than the voice of GOD's promise. The situation you are in is seasonal. SOON you will be out of that situation.

Change brings opportunities. Walk in your anointed authority instead of stooping in the shame of your past. Change often catalyses growth, presenting new opportunities that can lead to greater fulfillment. When you embrace the unknown, you open yourself up to experiences that challenge your perspectives and expand your horizons. Each shift in your circumstances can uncover pathways you had not considered, whether in your career, relationship, or personal aspiration. By navigating these transitions with an open mind, you not only adapt but also discover new passions and strengths. Ultimately, this journey through change fosters a more profound sense of contentment as you learn to appreciate the richness of life's unpredictability and the possibilities it brings, even during setbacks.

How content are you with...

- When you are handed a negative medical report, how do you balance your daily peace?

- Do you require coaching or therapy to change the ways that you are stuck in?

- Do you understand the correlation between happiness and contentment?

- Create a list of the things you had to let go of to find greater peace and contentment.

Habits for Satisfaction

Contentment Does Not Stem from Fame and Fortune

You either rule the day, or the day rules you. Eventually, life stumps you, your call, the fine line to contentment. Do yourself the definitive favour and take the time to recognise who you are, who you are beyond the commotion, façade, mask, and amusements. Purge your life of what's not serving you well. There is no more remarkable asset than knowing who you genuinely are. I am not what you say I am. I am what I overcame, and far more grit in my chromosomes. We all paint a story with precision. The whole world watched Prince Harry make some unsavoury choices in life. He has royal blood, yet he is human like the rest of us. He has limitations, the prince has habits, and the Duke of Sussex exhibits that contentment is not guaranteed within the confines of the palace.

*"Prince Harry has said he drank heavily, took drugs, and had panic attacks while struggling to cope with the pressures of royal life during his late 20s and early 30s. Harry discussed mental health with Oprah Winfrey in a wide-ranging interview. He spoke of the loss of his mother and said that as a child, he was **"so angry with what happened to her."** The Duke of Sussex, who was 12 when Princess Diana died in 1997, said that in the years that followed, few people around him discussed her death. Harry also revealed that he coped with panic attacks and severe anxiety as an adult.*

*Prince Harry has said that wearing a Nazi uniform at a fancy-dress party is **'one of the biggest mistakes of his life.'** The Duke of Sussex wore the deeply inappropriate outfit, in which he donned a red armband with a swastika, to a friend's costume party back in 2005. At the time, when images surfaced of the royal at the party and were printed in The Sun newspaper, there was an understandable widespread reaction of shock and shame towards Prince Harry. Harry said, **'I felt so ashamed afterwards. All I wanted to do was make it right.'**. The youngest son of King Charles III and Princess Diana also offered that he 'could have just ignored it and probably made the same mistakes over and over again,' but has instead 'learned from' the decision. **'I sat down and spoke to the chief rabbi in London, which had a profound impact on me. I went to Berlin and spoke to a Holocaust survivor.'"***

Fame + prestige + royalty do not equate to contentment. The history of Harry is supposed to indicate that despite all the amazing fortunes of this young man, he still had voids. Contentment eluded him. Paul from the Bible was content in all circumstances, and we are called to strive by his example. You are scuppered if you think it's a walk in the park. Even Prince Harry struggled. What radiates nobility is the fact that the Duke of Sussex did not allow his mistake to ruin him. He took the appropriate measures to find a remedy. Harry redefined his habits to see what satisfied him and what led him down a genuine path to contentment. We become what we stand for, what we say yes to, and most definitely what we say no to. You are a product of your environment. Harry is not ashamed of his flaws. He digs deep for genuine honesty; he earns respect, not just commands it. Yes, he changed for the better. Harry has a vision for whatever brings refinement, remedial, and progress, even though he is still filled with a million fragmented pieces; he has just readjusted them for an enhanced perspective.

Welcome to the New Version

Perhaps you are not recovering because you are trying to be who you were before the ordeal. Realise that, that person does not exist anymore. It's like holding on to water that is flowing downstream – that water has passed by, and it will never pass you by again. A new you has emerged; do not stifle the birth of your next version. Create a habit of always cheering and welcoming new versions of yourself. Breathe life into that person. Possibly, you look back and question the choices you have made, but it's unjust to chastise yourself for them. You cannot blame yourself for not knowing back then what you do know now. The reality is that you make each decision based on who you were at the time. As you advance, you think and do things differently. If you continue to stumble in the darkness, pieces of your soul will be neglected. Awaken to align to what produces contentment for you. Sometimes you get what you want. Other times, you get a lesson in endurance, technique, alignment, responsiveness, consideration, loyalty, diligence, resilience, humility, dependence, significance, attentiveness, defiance, commitment, transparency, heartache, and splendour. Whatever the example, eventually, you win when you have gleaned something. No matter what the circumstances are, always create a habit of learning something from experience.

Someday, whether you are 15, 30, or 70, you will stumble upon someone or something that will ignite a fire in you that will not expire. The delight begins when you accept that you cannot regulate other people's emotions or experiences. That's when you begin to live your authentic life. Some people will understand you; others will not. Some may result in controlling you like a puppet. What matters is that you live your definitive truth. Be compassionate, assist others, and never forget to live for yourself. May your heart always be at ease so we can glide into contentment every night as you slide into bed. Everyone is carrying their unknown past. Let introspection introduce you to the most intimate relationship with contentment. Altering your mind is not a symbol of evading reliability. It is frequently a sign of attaining perception. Comprehending you were incorrect does not mean you lack judgment. It means you lack insight. Development comes from remaining open to revising your views in the future. Cultivate a habit to develop constantly.

Make Peace with Your Journey

Construct harmony with the fact that the purpose of your life is not happiness but instead a journey of experience, capability, and progression. Happiness arrives as an organic consequence. When you are not chasing it as a vital objective, it will find its way to you. Ponder the facts of what you will attain in your life, career, and spiritual realm when you start to reframe the 'daily blues' and find joy in being content regardless of who serves what to you. My globe-trotting and travel nexus take me on many retail therapy sprees. I have shopped around the world and experienced a variety of personalities, accents, and currencies. One day, I found myself in Chanel, a prestigious brand – so naturally, I was expecting service that was top-notch. I was on a quest to purchase FOUR Chanel products, two as gifts. But the lady only gave me one gift bag. Technically, I deserved four, but she only threw in one more. I was not content with that. I could have taken my custom elsewhere. I thought, in the grand scheme of things, is it worth it? Sometimes, we want to fight tooth and nail to accomplish a principle, but at what cost? Two of the channel products were for me. The other two were gifts, and the two gift bags sufficed; not content, but the retail spree was adequate.

It's not quite a habit, but it's a standard I decided to live by. Your best self requires a continuous sacrifice of thoughts, habits, people, and places that don't align with who you are and where you are going. If you choose to be uncompromising constantly, it will be the labyrinth of your demise. Create a habit of choosing the path of least resistance, especially when those who are serving you are draped in apathy. It is a parody of power when you allow others to pickle your contentment with their mood or lack of service. The haven of contentment always lies in your hands. Train your mind to always understand this. Positivity is in the choices you make for yourself. Happiness depends on the quality of your decision and remember that joy does not come from ignoring the negative; it comes from overcoming the negative. When the wind changes direction, it unearths something that quenches you unconditionally.

Understand the Limitations that Others Have

Refrain from hurting the person that is unfairly serving you. Understand their limitations, their values, and edification. Put your strength in how you manage what is manipulated, mishandled, and misunderstood. Understand how things uttered in anger impair your equilibrium, a.k.a. contentment. When you feel overwhelmed and you need to find yourself, stop for a minute and examine your emotions. Remember to be present and live by your values even if you find yourself hidden under the emotional spectacle. Reach out and put your best foot forward. Behaving like someone else will erode your joy. You cannot control how other people behave, but you can control your response. Only when you deliberately choose to shine a light on someone else's darkness will you understand what contentment is. Pallid and gaunt expressions in attitude and action paint a real story of our contentment levels.

In 2022, the world saw this play out when Elon Musk served up change to his Twitter employees. The headlines lit up the news. *"RIP Twitter"* trended as employees resigned in the hundreds after Elon Musk's ultimatum. Twitter employees used the hashtag **#LoveWhereYouWorked** and the salute emoji as they tweeted about their resignations in protest of Elon Musk's latest ultimatum. Twitter was full of poignant messages from hundreds of employees of the social media platform who quit the company after an ultimatum from new owner Elon Musk. He demanded the staff to choose between being *"extremely hardcore"* and working intense, long hours or losing their jobs.

The taste of success spurs us on. The Twitter history mentioned above confirms that even when you are employed by a world gorilla, one of the wealthiest men on the planet, life has limits. The tongue-in-cheek hashtag denotes that contentment left the building in droves. Quitting your job indicates deficiencies that you are not willing to negotiate. Unconditional loyalty does not mean unconditional tolerance. Grasp that habits will walk you to a quiet place of genuine contentment. When you look back at the past, never dwell on the pain you felt; instead, ponder the strength you gained. Every day, people try to find their way over these complications; they measure their vitality towards contentment. It is a confrontation to feel unrecognised, concealed, and consumed, yet make every effort to shine the light to build a more extraordinary fortitude towards your authentic contentment.

People all over the world are trying to find their expression and generate a space for what is their most authentic selves inside their connections and their workplaces. It is a daunting task to navigate through insecurity and inequity while trying to chase contentment – there is no natural formula. Uncertainty is a killer for anything. It is vital to craft habits and practices and tap into tools to help you navigate through these circumstances. These will evolve with time based on your circumstances and progress; however, having the skills that will prepare you for success is the key.

Pap, Chakalaka, and boerewors are the traditional cuisines of South Africans. The local Indians love a pot of biryani and dhal or an authentic Durban bunny chow. Some lean towards the culinary pleasure of roti and stir-fried okra infused in garlic, copious amounts of onions, and fresh chilli, and garnished liberally with dhania. Yum, salivating = contentment. Just like our appetites and preferences, we all have different levels of satisfaction on the scene of culinary delights – so do life and the pocket of contentment. Some of us deal with the lousy hand dealt to us in a negative way that depicts defeat. You may even feel shanghaied. The remnants of dissatisfaction follow you like a shadow. Circumstances and emotions do not mark the path of contentment – you do, despite the unforeseen circumstances.

Be Certain When Uncertainty Strikes
Become adept at understanding the variation that is always served in life.

My brother, Jay, at 19, was at the prime of his life. He was living with zeal and threw caution to the wind. Suddenly, a force enveloped him in pain. Pain that cocooned him for several decades. Life became repugnant in every facet after the tragic accident at work that caused him to lose the use of his right hand and forever adopt the status of *"disabled."* I watched him grow into manhood with hatred strewn in every terrain of his life. He could not work, he could not find love, he did not marry, he had no children, his dreams were dormant, and society prejudged him. Life comes jam-packed with periods of flux. They could come masquerading as an accident, career change, medical diagnosis, death, divorce, fragmentation of a friendship, and global uncertainty.

We are all summoned to spread our well-toiled hands to the grind if we want to acquire some level of contentment. Sadly, the odds are stacked against some of us. Jay's human institution was shaken and never restored. Contentment was a fleeting aspiration. Withdrawal, compulsive behaviour, angst, and unhealthy choices became companions. He derailed every apparition he had for life. Uncertainty continues to soak itself in many lives daily. The options for a disabled person are bleak in South Africa in comparison to the options presented in the developed world. Life is not always as lush and green as Kikuyu grass, with the sky as blue as a Queensland topaz. Yet when forte is impossible, we are confronted to develop. How do you progress in a country that gives you no options on a silver platter? I'll be a monkey's uncle.

For three decades, I watched my brother Jay wade through life without any trace of contentment. He did not chase any guaranteed outcomes. During one of my sojourns to South Africa, I purchased a copy of Nick Vujicic's book, *Life Without Limits*. I hoped that this book would inspire him to live a more purposeful life. Nick was an Australian born without hands or legs; however, he is more than content. Nick carved out a future, found love, got married, had children, and created a legacy. One distinguishing thread between my brother and Nick is that Nick knows Jesus – who gave him an abundant life. Contentment has come to him on the tap. Regardless of which country we are born in, we are all tasked with becoming a better version of ourselves every day. Instead of asking why, dare yourself to modify, feel less incapacitated, and find your assurance towards contentment. It is an incredible feat despite what hand you are dealt with. Create a habit to flourish, not just endure.

"Man cannot discover new oceans unless he has the courage to lose sight of the shore." – Andre Gide. The pursuit of your purpose and insight requires COURAGE. Before you can see noticeable OUTCOMES, you habitually rely on the cosmos to hand you some luck with your name engraved on it. Where is your FAITH to carve out the dream and life that you deserve? Inconsistencies reduce the ease of your actions and the clarity of your feelings; create a habit to be consistent. You may have more than just TRUST in achieving what you set your mind to. Your supporters stand as one and clap on your progress.

You need to ACKNOWLEDGE that the keys to success and contentment are both in your hands. Do not become paranoid with the idea that the world is watching you. REFRAIN from the goldfish bowl syndrome. When you dwell in distress or insecurity and are challenged with the unspecified, MAGNIFY your capabilities, CHANGE, and DEVELOP new forms of yourself.

You ACQUIRE talents. You DOMINATE your expertise. You ignore the babble of overtures that the odds are stacked against you. Fair dinkum. Disappointments and setbacks entertain influential REALISATIONS. Welcome and herald the arrival of YOUR self-awareness. Emotions are neither black nor white; they are complicated, so be patient with yourself as you find yourself in the vortex. It's technically brilliant to take your time but never be stagnant – even if your resentment is mammoth.

Trust is the currency to drive value and loyalty; hoping that your life will turn the corner. You choose every mistake, so decide to learn from it. Both trivial and gigantic consequences fortify your SELF-BELIEF. You will become more CONFIDENT in yourself as you UNCOVER new experiences. Learn to discern the ominous signs of an impending storm and wend your way back to a safe path. You begin trusting the JOURNEY of arriving at our destination with the satisfaction that you purchased this ticket.

Separate Yourself from the Circumstances
History buffs and curious minds love to glean from the past and every hindrance. Irrespective of where you are currently and how bleak life may seem, take a moment to pause to acknowledge yourself for WHO YOU ARE and separate yourself from the circumstances. You are who your mind chooses to be, LIMITLESS and with a future. You manifest your life and future and BECOME continually every day with every thought, every action, and every decision. Your INACCESSIBLE visions may seem unreasonable, but it is VALID. Be loyal to that which exists within yourself. The hallmark of grace begins with you. Realisation is your only weapon. Look in the mirror and unleash it. You do not see the world as it is; you see it as you are. Do not see yourself as DISABLED. See yourself as having to work harder to achieve the same results as the rest of the world. Find your GRIT. You get to define your contentment with or without limitations.

In New Zealand, I have a goddaughter, Joycinda. She is an extraordinary young lass. I have gleaned so many profound lessons from her existence. She lost her mum during her birth. Death rewrites the ecosystem for the soul in many ways. In addition to the trammels of this horrendous protocol, Joycinda's life is full of blessings, and she has unconditional gratitude. In my book, *Don't Just Fly, SOAR*, I have included a card that I received from Joycinda when she was just a young child but so full of GRATITUDE. When injury and sundry take place, the heart sometimes grows heavy, and appreciation may loom lower on the gratefulness scale. You do not flourish when you build walls from your pain. When you are brave enough to navigate the waves of hope, then you master how to respond to life, and therein, gratitude is born in your hurt but pure heart. Make it a habit to be grateful despite your circumstances. Contentment will fall on you in bucket loads. When you are hurt and zoom out of your pain and help others, you create a coil of chain reaction for appreciation, gratitude, and contentment.

Research and Facts

Research indicates receiving gratitude improves cardiovascular stress responses and enhances resilience and routines. Gratitude expressions play a fundamental role in strengthening relationships. *"Oveis and co-authors tested the study participants' cardiovascular responses to stress on an individual and collaborative level. Both team members were monitored during the collaborative part of the experiment when they were designing the bicycle and creating a marketing plan. And individuals were monitored when one person out of the pair had to make the pitch before the panel of judges without looking or talking to their team member. During the collaborative task, control teams displayed threat responses marked by decreased blood flow and increased vascular constriction."*

However, a simple gratitude expression prior to the task eliminated these threat responses. During the individual product pitches, control teams showed modest challenge responses marked by vascular dilation and increased blood flow to the periphery. However, gratitude – expressing teams showed significantly larger, amplified challenge responses, which aided their performance.

Gratitude expressions within work environments perhaps are the key to managing your day-to-day stress responses. Ponder how this will correlate to filling up your contentment tank. The tuneful sound of music infuses calmness. Gratitude plants better health and enhances resilience, which is ingenious. Contentment comes in all shapes and sizes. The blind will of life will spill every day. One day, realisation will sprout. Generate a habit of thinking outside the square sooner rather than later.

In December 2022, the world watched in shock and dismay as the renowned Stephen Twitch Boss left a suicide note at a motel, alluding to challenges in the past, and turned his phone to aeroplane mode before shooting himself dead. He was a sought-after dancer. He was Ellen DeGeneres Show's DJ, dancer, co-host, and co-executive producer. He was second-to-none choreographer. No doubt he found both fame and fortune, but something was amiss to resort to suicide. Whatever may shatter and punch you, it does not just pounce on you. It starts with the little levels of contentment that you allow to slip, and eventually, you are staring down an abyss, not sure how you reached there and how to find your way back. I charted this path where I saw no hope but only one option to end it all, but soon clarity arrived, and I knew I had to find my level of satisfaction in the simple daily things before I could master my big dreams. Life is full of nuances and contradictions; the solutions are in your hands. Your future depends on how you experience the essence of life here and now. **If you or a loved one requires help, call LIFELINE for confidential mental health support. If you find it difficult to open and speak to a person, try talking to God. Rest assured that He hears you. Here are some scriptures to help you.**

Circle of Contentment

Life Experience

To be able to maintain the wholesomeness of life before a trauma redefines you is not an easy path. Even the most determined of us must combat the sincere moods of misery and sadness. It is unwise to pretend that this life is served up with no complications. Our predicament often defines our character as what we've gone through, enabling us to become who we are meant to be. Sometimes, the light at the end of the tunnel is dimming, and you no longer possess the strength to keep going. I reached this point, and clarity circled me back. My debut book, *Don't Just Fly, SOAR*, has impacted people around the world. I could not have made this difference in so many lives if I had lost sight of my contentment with all the cards on the table of my life. Situations may redefine you but never allow them to change your destiny. Circumstances do change with the progression of time; give yourself time to heal. Never decide that you cannot reverse. You have no idea how much you encourage someone just by existing and having the opportunity to share your setbacks and comebacks.

Allow yourself the grace to understand that this moment will not define you. It is merely an obstacle, a stepping stone towards a solution that right now may be unforeseen. Your uniqueness is vital to everyone who encounters you. The world is a better place because you add something exclusive to it. Your presence matters, and you make a distinction. Even in your intimate, bleakest moments, understand that happiness will re-emerge. Life is made up of storms, rain, sunshine, floods, and rainbows. Do not give up in one season without waiting for the change. Don't ever give up; contentment will creep in when you choose it.

Life has a community of solvers; form a habit of reaching out when you are overwhelmed and lack contentment. Chew the cud if you must, but never make the mistake of feeling alone and having no help. Everything is interconnected: joy, fear, hate, envy, revenge, spite, loneliness, anxiety, depression, and even kindness. It all finds a way to a root cause. Become a professional beggar and contest for your life and satisfaction of it. Come out valorous with tears and scars. *"Many people will panic to find a charger before their phone dies but will not panic to find a plan before their dream dies."* – Elon Musk. Instead of panicking for your soul, understand when your soul is deprived. Your soul is disadvantaged when it lacks truth. Your soul is deprived when it needs sincerity. Your soul is destitute when it is crying out for authenticity and integrity. Your soul is unprivileged when it desires nothing but unconditional love. These are the common threads to contentment. Invent a habit of charging your soul, not just your phone.

If you lose something or someone, break the tradition of what you used to do together. After divorce, death, birthday, and anniversary, cultivate a new habit. Find pleasure in something new. Life is full of decisions that will lead you to contentment. Select to be decisive. Most of us make decisions accidentally – why? Choose to be better, not bitter. Life is not about perfection; it is about experience and growth. Elect to be a person of fine calibre and principle. Contentment will marinate your soul when you choose to do what's right, especially when no one is watching. Develop the habit of drinking water from the brook where impalas drink. Animals will never drink bad water. Make your bed among the roses but be aware of the thorns. When you eat what was tarnished by a caterpillar, then you have ascertained it is not poisonous for your mind and soul as well. Confidently harvesting mushrooms where insects convene; indicates they have found something valuable. Plant where the mole digs – your effort will not be in vain, and you will reap a harvest.

The different states of yoghurt – smooth, thick, runny, or chunky – serve as a metaphor for the varied stages of personal growth and emotional well-being. Just as yoghurt undergoes fermentation and transformation, our experiences shape us too. The process of creating balance and flexibility mirrors the journey of finding relevance in your life without or with achieving contentment. Sometimes, you might feel like runny yoghurt, lacking firmness or direction, yet this state can foster adaptability and openness to new experiences. Conversely, a thick, creamy yoghurt represents stability and grounding, offering comfort but potentially leading to complacency.

Finding relevance among these states involves embracing the fluctuations of life. Each phase – whether smooth or lumpy – offers lessons. Instead of seeking constant contentment, you can focus on the growth that arises from discomfort and change, much like yoghurt evolving through fermentation. This perspective encourages us to appreciate the process, understanding that relevance can thrive even in states of unease, leading to deeper insights and a richer existence.

Consume from the wholesome basket; you will have a healthier disposition. Connect with nature often, sleep under the stars, and swim in the deep blue ocean – let every worry wash off. Unload your thoughts and burdens until you become light as a feather flickering in the wind. Observe more than offering solutions with limited experience – sit back and learn a thing or two before you wear the hat of the master. Contentment will find you when you practice this model. We live in a time when it's more dramatic to lose your phone than your soul – align with what truly matters, and contentment will chase you down. *"Every bit of pain that you have experienced in your life was currency, whether you acknowledge it or not, so you may as well buy something incredible with it."* – Tyler Perry. Create a habit of listening to someone who you think has nothing in common with you, then learn something new. Some are naturally anointed as arrogant but have no idea why contentment eludes them; you always have a choice.

The Art of Contentment
The art of contentment, as expressed in the wisdom of the Scripture, invites us to embrace a state of peace regardless of our circumstances. It teaches us that true contentment arises not from external conditions but from inner resilience and gratitude. By focusing on what we have rather than what we lack, we cultivate a heart that is anchored in trust and appreciation. This mindset enables us to navigate life's challenges with grace, recognising that every situation holds potential for growth and learning. Ultimately, contentment becomes a practice of being present and finding joy in the simplicity of life. In Matthew 6:31, *"Therefore do not be anxious, saying, what shall I eat? Or what shall I drink?"* This scripture confirms to us we should be anxious about nothing and find contentment in all circumstances.

How content are you with...

- When you are hurt, do you have someone to talk to?

- Do you learn from your mistakes and take steps to correct them?

- In what ways do you express gratitude?

- How do you prompt your disabilities to set you up for success or contentment?

Practice Prepares You for Success

The Bible confirms that due to the crowds that had come to Bethlehem, there was no room at the inn for Mary and Joseph (Luke 2:7). Jesus was born at night, in a stable. After Jesus was delivered, Mary, His mother, wrapped Him in cloth and laid Him in a manger.

So, why was the Saviour and King born in a place where animals were kept? And why was He then laid in the animals' food trough? Surely, God's Son deserved a high-profile birth, in the most elegant of surroundings. But, instead, God's own Son made His appearance on earth in the lowest of circumstances. This humble birth conveys an amazing message to creation: the transcendent God condescended to come to us. Instead of coming to earth as a pampered, privileged ruler, Jesus was born in meekness, as one of us. He is approachable, accessible, and available – no palace gates bar the way to Him; no ring of guards prevents our approach. The King of Kings came humbly, and His first bed was a manger. Mary, His mother, was content with this. Jesus himself was satisfied. There was no selfie frenzy, gender reveal, or social media update, yet the three wise men showed up. The news trended without any marketing budget. Something prevailed…

This well-known history collapsed the moral framework for a pecking order to drive importance. God came to earth with no frills and glam. Why does society confront humans with disdain when they do not charm the world with the fragrance of prosperity? We have created illusions and fracas that we cling to, creating a greater gap on the contentment scale. Everyone needs to measure up. Measure up to what? Your standards or the model of Jesus? You daily apply your perceptions with alacrity. Flowers have their language in their silence; they convey so much, and humans convey so much in spoken and unspoken ways – not one is picturesque. When you smell the scent of life, then you learn to triumph over what's within you, and then what's around you will never faze you.

I recently came around a table where a person lied to me several times, abused me, and caused me incomprehensible trauma. Yet the discussion was centred around how this narcissist acts as a victim to my reactions. The others around the table demanded that I ignore all the indiscretions and still show respect because that is what God says. It certainly was a round table with buffoons. No command of the word of God nor self-love and self-respect. Self-love is a state of appreciation for oneself that grows from actions that support our physical, psychological, and spiritual growth. Self-love means having a high regard for your well-being and happiness. Self-love means taking care of your needs and not sacrificing your well-being to please others. Self-respect is proper respect for oneself as a human being, and regard for one's standing or position.

Self-respect can be challenging to practice if you are a people – pleaser. The fear of saying no can keep you stuck in a cycle of abandoning your needs and giving in to things that don't serve you. When we allow others to take advantage of us, we chip away at our self-esteem, which leads to more angst, less interpersonal efficiency, and depreciates our self-respect. Even those of us who practice interpersonal effectiveness find ourselves in situations that can prompt us to give away our self-respect. No matter how hurt you are and how difficult it is, never let anyone corrode your boundaries. Dismantling your self-love and self-respect will decompose your journey to contentment.

At this round table discussion, I noticed that I was about to let people take advantage of me. But I asserted myself to bring my self-worth to the table. I was hurt immensely, but I walked stronger than before. Each time you stand up for what's just, you respect yourself.

When others take advantage of you, it can generate anger, which may lead to:

- Uncompromising reactions and aggressive outbursts.

- Emotions of incompetence and fortifying the false belief that you do not merit respect.

- Aptly ignites you to feel self-awareness and aids you to act boldly. This will help you cultivate robust self-esteem and more self-respect; it takes ample practice and leads to appealing outcomes.

Standing up for yourself can feel uncomfortable, but it pays dividends. When you begin this cycle and develop boundaries, you learn to value yourself and your self-worth. Boundaries are beyond important in the development of self-respect. Some people are an institution of themselves for demanding how others treat them with no consideration of what they bring to the equation. How does it feel to be treated unfairly? How does this make you feel? Reflect and understand your emotions. Do not negotiate your worth with anyone. Your value dwells in your heart. Live it. You can get away with adding straw for so long, and then you cannot. Get defiant about insults to your soul. A requiem to the bygone helps to move forward to a new season. Everyone appreciates a fresh meal rather than leftovers. Think coherently and create organic connections that enhance your self-worth. Pay attention to the details – does your network act with integrity? Do they display more pride with doses of ego rather than seeking to keep their self-respect intact?

To develop self-respect, you must act on it. You show others how you want to be treated by your actions and words. Show them that you are valuable by speaking up and setting strong boundaries. When you have a captive audience, there is no introduction required; the same analogy is applicable when you have a grounded foundation with self-respect, then contentment flows on. Refrain from allowing any trivia to deter you from what brings you ultimate joy. Occasionally, self-love is not about admiring yourself. Sometimes self-love is also not about being your cheerleader. Understand the distinctions.

Don't trade your authenticity for approval. Self-love means that we should jeer deeper. Invigorating your heart, unwrapping the layers. It's about having the audacity to look at the bits of yourself that you don't like and unpacking the reason as to why. Sometimes self-love is having the courage to be honest with yourself and paying attention to the mistakes you made, the areas you need to grow within, and how you hope to change. Sometimes self-love means having the courage to admit your failures and then forgive yourself for making them, too. You should love yourself. You should lift yourself. You should cultivate a relationship within your body, mind, heart, and soul that is rooted in admiration, affirmation, and love.

When the heart breaks into many pieces, a day can feel like a lifetime. Use your tools and your wisdom to shield your self-respect. Assess what's not working in your life, physical health, work, relationships, mental health, and the whole gamut. Self-reflection is a necessary component of progress. When you are disgruntled in your relationships, or they do not confidently fuel your sense of worth. This is most definitely a red flag for your self-love and respect. Authentic connection requires elbow grease. Others will not love or respect you if you do not love and respect yourself first. Sometimes the world is too busy to notice your void. You need to champion your path. Seek the balm to your soul. I read, take reflective walks, listen to music, and articulate myself with my expressive pen, writing and a massage. Realign your inner compass.

Fragmented pieces of life are difficult to navigate; however, so much equity originates and spurs self-respect. From the ashes, beauty is crafted. In those tears, you learn to sink, swim, or drown. Those intense sentiments create your personal brute; your heartbreak teaches you new ways to love, and that rejection harnesses you to accept others. You can trace nuances in a heartbeat. This is the story that tells you self-love is like the rock of Gibraltar. Empathy is your companion, and you understand the circumstances even from the unspoken words. You know how to dish out self-respect to yourself and others. Contentment reflects your self-worth, self-love, and self-respect.

In the multi-award-winning book, *No Friend but the Mountain*, the author Behrouz Boochani narrates captivating non-fiction history. This is a well known book in Australia. The author remained exiled on Manus Island during the launch of this book. I am certain this book does not encapsulate all the emotions that the author and the rest of the refugees experienced on this island. Kurdish, Persian, Aboriginal, Australian, Sri Lankan, and Sudanese brands with different views and rules for life, but the heart utilities are the same. You cannot breathe new breaths into old mindsets or new acquaintances. Behrouz tells the gut wrenching story of seeking asylum as an illegal refugee. He comes on board a rotten boat from Indonesia – he has not eaten for days. He finds a single pistachio on the deck of the boat; it is covered in grease. He grabs it, wipes it, and consumes it as an award-winning culinary delight.

The boat sinks, and many souls perish; he is rescued with a few others. Eventually, they set foot on dry land, excited. A new federal law has come into effect in Australia, and illegal refugees arriving via boat are banished to Manus Island. Boochani is malnourished and bemused. He recounts many inhumane acts inflicted on humans who are simply seeking a better life. No doubt food is scarce, and emotions are high. What captures my attention is the fact that even in a state of starvation, the author chooses his dignity over necessity. He has found his contentment, and it resides in the depths of his heart despite his negative circumstances. Routinely, the Australian offices overseeing the refugees lavish the impoverished with a cake. This luxury creates a frenzy for the starving...

"Sometimes the force of the crowd is so great that the officer loses balance and almost falls over. To stay up, he has no choice but to throw the box metres away with all its contents inside. They swarm towards the box, and all the pieces of the cake have scattered over the ground. During these moments, the prisoners are transformed into something way beyond sheep – maybe more like a group of predatory wolves, hungry wolves in the middle of winter, transformed into starving wolves pouncing on the prey with no mercy. But I never went towards the officer to get any cake. On no occasion did I ever take even a step in the direction of the mayhem. It's not that I am an extremely proud person. It's not even that I want to maintain my humanity when faced with the option of behaving like a sheep. No. I swear, it is nothing like that; there is no reason for making my proud decision, a decision made during moments when my appetite governs my soul. What influences my decision is the feeling of weakness that takes hold of me. My body is faint; I am just like a hungry fox. I imagine this feeling to be evidence of maintaining my basic sense of what it is to be human. From the very first moment when the officer begins his kind gesture, I know I am an animal that has already lost the game. For this reason, I will always watch the spectacle from a distance."

Cleaving to the demands of convention even when death is at the door, is the ultimate model of contentment in the face of adversity. I was in tears when I read this initially for the victims and then for those that are in charge. I could never be content doing a job where I take solace in degrading the human spirit to this calibre. Love and death may come uninvited, but dignity and contentment are in your hands. This refugee models it to us so aptly. Dreams vanish, and wake up to reality, and yet you can control your contentment tank with precision. In Julius Caesar, Shakespeare depicts to us appropriately the realisations of fate versus free will. Cassius refuses to accept Caesar's rising power and deems a belief in fate to be nothing more than a form of passivity or cowardice. He says to Brutus, *"Men, at some time, were masters of their fates. The fault, dear Brutus, is not in our stars. But in ourselves, we are underlings."* Based on the skill, the individual contentment can still be attained and mastered. It is okay if your vigour looks a little different in each season. What you nourish will grow.

Guaranteed, there are different answers to happiness, well-being, and contentment. Sometimes we think the situation is unbearable, and often it is, yet some individuals find the capacity to rise to new heights. We are all not sailing in the same boat. Perhaps we are in the same storm. Certain individuals have racing yachts, a substantial number have tinnies, considerable members of society have canoes, a significant selection of this cohort has a luxury liner cruising the uncharted waters, and a generous sum are simply drowning. Is contentment relative to your situation?

Before Jim Kwik was recognised as one of the foremost experts in speed reading, memory improvement, brain performance, and accelerated learning – and a highly sought-out trainer for top organisations like Virgin, Nike, Zappos, NYU, GE, Fox Studios, Harvard, and Singularity University – Jim was known as *"the boy with the broken brain. At the age of five, Jim suffered a head injury that left him with severe learning challenges, and as a result, he struggled throughout his schooling years. He read considerably slower. He absorbed and understood less. And learning anything new was an uphill battle.*

Hoping to compensate for these challenges, Jim doubled down on his efforts in college in hopes of staying on par with his peers. But spending hours in the library, single-mindedly focused on his studies, came at a cost. He hardly ate. He hardly slept. In a dangerously weakened state, weighing only 117 pounds, Jim passed out, fell down a flight of stairs, and once again sustained further head injuries. Jim woke up in the hospital two days later. It was during his recovery in the hospital that he had the epiphany that would change the entire trajectory of his life. It occurred to him that his entire education revolved around being taught what to learn – math, science, geography, and Spanish. But never once was he taught how to learn.

This single thought became his obsession. As Jim began to unravel how the human brain really works, he developed strategies to dramatically enhance his mental performance. And as he saw more success, he began teaching his newfound techniques to his fellow students, which would later become his life mission. For the last 25+ years, Jim has dedicated his life to helping others unleash their true genius and brainpower to learn anything faster and live a life of greater power, productivity, and purpose."

What a testament: two traumatic brain injuries. One as a child and one as an adult, yet Jim was not content to accept what life dished out to him. Science confirms we can create new brain cells, and as you grow older, you can learn faster. Jim did not allow his diagnosis to define him or confine his level of contentment. Cheating death until it finds you – some live by that mantra, while others leave no stone unturned to find refinement. Dedicated navel-gazing will take you nowhere noticeable. Jim models to us that in the valley of injury and despair, he found a formula to transcend his life. Neuroscience is real. Tap into it if you want to flourish with contentment. Be courageous. Take a chance. Nothing can replace experience. Spend time with someone who you perceive to have nothing in common with. Make the effort to learn from the young and the old – Google does not have all the answers. Sometimes you need to tap into your intuition and build your fortitude to find your contentment.

Creating a positive outlook will pave your way to contentment. Living a life in the limelight comes with expected challenges; will anyone ever find a thread of contentment in this arena? We are flaunted with distorted perceptions and media propaganda. There is no mysterious logic to the paparazzi that reigns supreme. The chronic dysfunction keeps the circus going. People do not see the world as it is; they see it as they are; hence, the reporting standards are not defined by industry standards. So how do you find contentment when your life is plastered all over the tabloids and you must discover elements of your life via the tabloids? This can be rough terrain. Society may view these things as imperfections, but they are not; they are memories that bind us. Due to a diverse array of causes, the world watched in dismay as *Prince Harry and Meghan* stepped away from royal duties.

"The saying usually goes that you can't know what happens behind closed doors. But thanks to Prince Harry and Meghan Markle's new documentary, Harry & Meghan, the world now has a pretty good idea. The door in question? One at Sandringham, where on January 13, 2022, Prince Harry, Prince William, Prince Charles, and then reigning monarch Queen Elizabeth II discussed the Duke and Duchess of Sussex's future in the royal family. Days earlier, the couple had released an explosive Instagram statement saying they were to 'step back' from their duties. After that private meeting concluded, it turned out that 'back' really meant 'down,' as on January 18, Buckingham Palace released a statement declaring that Harry and Meghan were 'no longer working members of the Royal Family.'"

Even with the methodological rigour of each life, we can never understand all the facts; the media only offers a fraction of the story. Vastly embellished with propaganda – to sell at all costs despite the truth. No, the media does not take into consideration the subject matter's level of contentment, emotional well-being, and general ethics. Anyone is fair game for raking in the money. Despite being a visual delight to the camera and lighting up social media, these subjects are humans. No person can acquire contentment when their brand, persona, and personal and public life are dissected and thrown to the public to devour. Everyone paints perceived affronts at some point in their life; guaranteed, if you were living like a goldfish in a glass bowl, you would find it suffocating as well. Yet the public is consistent at throwing daggers at people they have any affiliation with. Have you stopped to ponder how these people reach their levels of contentment? Which is so eloquently prescribed by the media and then dispensed by the public. The fundamental question is, why are you a pawn in the equation to murder contentment?

Relent in a particular direction, but never distance the context. Keep it real. Do not dish out if you cannot handle the same dose of medicine yourself. When you are mature, you will arrive at two certainties in life:

1. Does it benefit positively, causing no harm?
2. Does it pay dividends now and in the future?

Your conduct reflects your reputation; you may gain contentment from sticking a needle in someone's eye. Before you do that, ensure your closet is free of skeletons. When the mirror is held up to you, rest assured your level of contentment will be beleaguered. Stop the tall poppy syndrome, especially when you do not belong in the arena. Refrain from dehumanising people. Their contentment in life is just as important as yours, period. Gain a stalwart virtue to live by. *"Competition is the law of the jungle, but cooperation is the law of civilization."* – Peter Kropotkin. The greatest conundrum of life – you will never be certain about who is imploring you and who is hustling you. You have a material differentiator in your hands; use it. Shed off the actions of traditionalism that have suffocated you consciously and then unconsciously choked others. If you fit the status of flawlessly groomed, fortunately resilient, mercifully controlled, and model a perfected demeanour, then cast the first stone.

With reference to Harvard Business Review, you can build daily work habits that support your mental health, and this will ultimately increase your contentment quotient. *"When you're struggling with your mental health, getting through the workday can feel more difficult. Tending to your mental health at work is critical – whether you've been diagnosed with a specific condition. Here are some ways to make your workday work for your mental health.*

"First, establish strong habits around deep work. Building a consistent routine for focused work will help you feel a little more in control of your life and schedule. For instance, scheduling deep work from 10 AM to noon daily can help automate your productivity patterns, making them more manageable – even on days when you're feeling off.

Then, create routines to manage tasks without immediate deadlines. It's easy to spend your workdays focusing on one urgent task after another. But when you work that way, less immediate responsibilities slip through the cracks and pile up, causing incremental stress. Setting aside regular times to tackle non-urgent work can help you stay on top of your overall workload.

Finally, schedule unfocused time. It's not possible to be locked in and undistracted all day, every day. Balancing focused work with periods of unstructured time can enhance your ability to think creatively and problem solve. After intense work sessions, taking a walk or reading casually can help you clear your mind and recover."

Don't give someone else the privilege to make you happy or unhappy.

Reserve that prerogative for yourself. You must find contentment even in the mundane. It involves shifting your perspective to appreciate the simple moments of daily life. By practicing mindfulness and gratitude, you can discover joy in routine tasks, seeing them as opportunities for reflection and connection. Embracing the ordinary helps cultivate a deeper sense of fulfillment, reminding one that happiness often resides in the smallest experiences. All these experiences contribute to a bigger picture and ultimately to your level of contentment. Never despise the humble path.

How content are you with...

- How do you manage the mundane circumstances?
- Do you consciously or unconsciously affect another person's level of contentment?
- How would you feel if someone else managed your contentment tank?
- Do you promote external forces to define your contentment?

Expectation Versus Reality

Discernment is the key when it comes to business and personal decisions. *"Never respond to the shade of a tree that does not bear fruit – translation:* **Don't pay attention to those who are critical of your life and choices when their own lives are not producing anything good."** – **Unknown.** Ascertain how to establish healthy boundaries so your contentment will not be corrupted by those you allow to influence you. Discernment is the sparkle of the heart, making its way down the cheeks of a weather worn and life-lived face that is filled with a well-weighed journey and lived experience. So many people make decisions that change the trajectory of life in either a positive or negative fashion. Rubber hits the road when you learn to be content with your expectations versus the reality of your outcome.

Societies' sentiments are often deliberations of their own filters and prognosis. They may have very little to do with you or an incident. Constantly remember every choice you have – make it from the chambers of your heart and with peace that offers contentment. We do not have a crystal ball to confirm how the future will pan out; however, we do have discernment, professional expertise, and intuition. Contentment can vanish if you make the wrong decision. History offers us many lessons.

"No two tech executives are quite as enigmatic and private as Google co-founders Larry Page and Sergey Brin. The two men, who started Google more than 20 years ago while they were computer science graduate students at Stanford University, have hardly been seen or heard from in the last half-decade or so since restructuring the company to create Google parent Alphabet and leaving Sundar Pichai in charge of a newly streamlined Google. In fact, Page and Brin tried to sell Google for $1 million to internet portal company Excite in 1999, as recalled by Khosla Ventures founder Vinod Khosla. The prominent venture capitalist was able to negotiate Page and Brin down to as low as $750,000 but Excite CEO George Bell still wouldn't take the deal."

No doubt there was a level of contentment with the historic thread of Google. Firm in commitment and truly inspired by competition. These innovators offer us much to ruminate. How have you mastered your level of expectation? When you are faced with a life-changing decision, do you trace your heartbeat for contentment? Are you able to live with the outcome? Contentment dwells in between expectation and reality. What comes to the surface when you make the wrong decision? Do you let contentment persistently evade you? You cannot stop the rain by asking it to stop; sometimes, you must let the circumstances prevail. You must develop the art of tearing the shroud of uncertainty and not allowing it to govern you or your future. Stand your ground in questioning anticipation but be content when your decision plummets south. Take ownership of the outcome before it arrives so you can deal with either a positive or negative result.

Never permit your persuasion to be emphasised by the collective stance of grey; sitting on the fence and playing with fate may rob you of contentment as well. Pick a side, then punctuate that with skillset, awareness, acumen, and confidence. Life will take on a new stature when you choose the pictures that you want to paint rather than letting the paint randomly fall on the canvas. You get to create this masterpiece – your one audacious life. Gleaning the craftsmanship to make decisions that lead to your personal contentment is discovering the process of christening your soul and clarifying your heart. Regardless of your decision being right or wrong, you require experience to develop. If you choose not to grow, then you have opted to stagnate. This may create repressed potent toxins that turn into morbidity, misery, or vicious deeds. Your narrative may be complicated, but nothing is more challenging than spending your entire life running from it. Get familiar with your liabilities, take calculated risks, and understand your options. Only when you are courageous enough to survey the dusk will you uncover the vast command of the dawn.

In 2019, during my sojourn to South Africa, I was blessed to attend the Andrea Bocelli concert in Johannesburg. It was a life-changing experience as goosebumps covered me and my soul resonated with ambience. Despite all the voids in life, I felt perceptible contentment. Music traces a pattern in the mind that lingers after the music moves on. The memory holds that prompting and the composer count on your capacity to do so. Thus, you confirm the designed outcome. Like words in a sentence, we encounter music as moments in linear succession. The array is relaxed or compelling by design, like configurations in architecture or decoration in interior design – perhaps some muted tones but stunning. A cappella but captivating Bocelli indeed owns this.

"Andrea Bocelli is an Italian tenor. He was born visually impaired with congenital glaucoma, and at the age of 12, Bocelli became completely blind following a brain haemorrhage resulting from a football accident. After performing evenings in piano bars and competing in local singing contests, Bocelli signed his first recording contract with the Sugar Music label. He rose to fame in 1994, winning the 44th Sanremo Music Festival, performing 'Il mare calmo della sera.'"

Since 1994, Bocelli has recorded 15 solo studio albums of both pop and classical music, three greatest hits albums, and nine complete operas, selling over 75 million records worldwide. In 1998, Bocelli was named one of People magazine's 50 Most Beautiful People. He duetted with Celine Dion on the song "The Prayer" for the animated film Quest for Camelot, which won the Golden Globe Award for Best Original Song and was nominated for the Academy Award for Best Original Song. In 1999, he was nominated for Best New Artist at the Grammy Awards. He captured a listing in the Guinness Book of World Records with the release of his classical album Sacred Arias, as he simultaneously held the top three positions on the US Classical Albums charts.

"Bocelli was made a Grand Officer of the Order of Merit of the Italian Republic in 2006 and was honoured with a star on the Hollywood Walk of Fame on 2 March 2010 for his contribution to Live Theatre, and he was awarded a Gold Medal for Merit in Serbia in 2022. Singer Celine Dion has said that 'if God would have a singing voice, he must sound a lot like Andrea Bocelli' and record producer David Foster has often described Bocelli's voice as the most beautiful in the world."

Rhythms, melodies, tunes, crescendos, and harmonies express to us the relevance of music to our souls. Music can change the mode of your life. In an instant, you can be transformed from a foul mood to tapping your feet to a beat. Synchronisations are dramatic with grief and joy. Melody and undeviating harmony, when merged with rhythm and an unforgettable voice, create an experience that the ears heed but the soul computes. Music has the power to affect the soul in a philosophical manner. The contours of the melody generate a channel of communication – a language between the performer and listener. Just as linguistic metaphors exist, we also have musical metaphors. Blaring unexpected bursts that may infer fury, melodies can be described as relaxed, smooth, warm, rigid, or curious. It leads you to contentment or takes you to a place you want to run from – that's powerful.

Bocelli was born with a health impairment, yet this did not define nor confine him. He found contentment in his incomplete portion. He is blind, but he still feels the beauty of the sun. The most influential and applied changes occur when you decide to take control of what you can control. Instead of yearning to regulate what you cannot. Remember, you cannot switch fate, but you can adjust yourself. Do not be afraid because your terrain is vastly different. When you go through the inferno, you will come out on the other side, and you will find a greater version of yourself. Do not live a life that reflects you are undeserving, despised, or lacking just because you did not fit a mould. Despite the deficiency, Andrea Bocelli set the world on fire. Kudos and accolades found him despite his limitations. Bocelli models to us that contentment begins from within. When life is packaged with punitive battles, we tend to offer a finer message to the world. We become our strongest in the weakest place – contentment is a dexterity, not a birthright.

Authentic contentment is a well-established sense of accepting who and where you are at any given moment under any circumstance. We frequently get so ingrained in our distracted lives that we hardly pay attention to living in the moment. When you finally emerge from the maze, focus on your blue sky – where do you want to be in the future? The dictionary defines contentment as *"the state of being mentally or emotionally satisfied with things as they are."* It is rare that we find anyone who is truly content with his or her condition in life. I recall being on vacation and getting dressed to go out for dinner. Both my friend and I were in the bathroom getting our hair done. She had blonde hair that was pin straight, and she was curling her hair. I had naturally curly brunette hair, and I was straightening my hair. Eventually our eyes met in the mirror, and we both burst out laughing, exclaiming how we wish we had each other's hair. Often, we believe we will be satisfied if we have the opposite of what we have.

The Bible has a blueprint about contentment – being satisfied with what you have, who you are, and where you are headed. Jesus said, *"Therefore I tell you, do not worry about your life, what you will eat or drink, or about your body, what you will wear. Is not life more important than food, and the body more important than clothes?"* – Matthew 6:25. In essence, Jesus is telling us to be content with what we have. The apostle Paul was a man who suffered and went without the comforts of life more than most people could ever imagine (2 Corinthians 11:23-28). Yet He knew the secret of contentment: *"I know what it is to be in need, and I know what it is to have plenty. I have learned the secret of being content in any and every situation, whether well fed or hungry, whether living in plenty or in want. I can do everything through Him who gives me strength."* A meme that reads, *"He with the most toys wins!"* exemplifies the world's desires for more and then some more.

Dopamine is one of the *"feel good"* chemicals in our brain. Interacting with the pleasure and reward centre of our brain, dopamine – along with other chemicals like serotonin, oxytocin, and endorphins – plays a vital role in how happy we feel. In addition to our mood, dopamine also affects movement, memory, and focus. Healthy levels of dopamine drive us to seek and repeat pleasurable activities, while low levels can have an adverse physical and psychological impact. When the brain has a healthy level of dopamine, we feel good. Our motivation increases. We are productive. We plan well. We learn quickly. We are driven, excited about life, focused, and attentive. Healthy levels of dopamine can also make us more social and extroverted. This *"feel good"* neurotransmitter also helps increase our empathy for others, making us more willing to adapt to someone else's need(s).

Dopamine levels impact mood regulation, muscle movement, sleep patterns, the ability to store and recall memories, concentration, appetite, and the ability to express self-control. When there is an imbalance in this chemical, a person cannot function at an optimal level. Low dopamine levels, also called *"dopamine deficiency,"* can make us feel fatigued and restless. There are many ways we can naturally increase our dopamine levels. Engaging in healthy lifestyle practices can be one of the easiest ways to naturally increase dopamine levels. Exercise, massage, meditation, gardening, reading, or even playing with a pet can help increase dopamine levels. Getting regular, good-quality sleep can also help keep our dopamine levels balanced.

According to a study investigating the effects of music on dopamine, people who listened to instrumental songs elicited an emotional response and had a 9% increase in brain dopamine levels. Science consistently shows that low exposure to sunshine can reduce levels of mood-boosting neurotransmitters, including dopamine. Similarly, spending more time outdoors and increasing sunlight exposure can help raise dopamine levels. Balancing your health, diet, spirituality, and mental wellness all enhances your level of contentment.

Did your contentment train ever derail because you did not have a cordial close? Unmatched loyalty can create contention and reside in your heart even if you choose not to accept it. End the bond before it oozes resentment and devastation. Understand how the undercurrent really operates and develop your superpower to gain influence and make informed choices. You cannot rise like a phoenix after every treachery – you will lose some battles. Select your battles with precision. Detachment does not mean hatred; it means aligning with something that meets your values. Understand the risk that might present when you walk away from people who see you as a threat. When you have good intentions, you will attract people around you who have good intentions as well. Remember not to throw stones when you dwell in a glass house.

Imagine if a couple was dating, and he wanted to marry this woman. As any conventional woman, she finds merit in his character and agrees with a caveat that he untangles from his past relationships and breaks away from all the baggage. After marriage, if the wife discovers that her husband is still in a relationship with his ex-girlfriend, every trace of contentment will evaporate from the marriage. The husband will need to create equity to sustain the marriage; if not, both husband and wife will never reach a point of satisfaction. Most humans will naturally steer towards self-justification, especially when they consciously make the wrong decision. Cognitive dissonance is when a person holds two cognitions that are psychologically inconsistent. It may be as simple as trying to please both your wife and girlfriend. A healthy mind understands this equation as complex and will refrain from indulging in it. The husband will reduce dissonance by convincing himself that having a girlfriend is not harmful or unethical. When you are trapped in between two moral forces, understand that you will never reap contentment.

The husband's extracurricular activities may create repercussions in his marriage. The onus is upon him to find threads of ultimate satisfaction. The wife has the obligation to herself to trace what cultivates her level of contentment without any mental justifications. The moment you feel like you must prove your worth to someone is the time you need to walk away. You will never find contentment in an equation where you must substantiate who you are and what you are worthy of. Any opportunity to cheat shines the light on your level of integrity, regardless of how much effort you put into self-justification. Moral choices are the cathedrals of life that will invite contentment into your life. When you consciously choose cognitive dissonance, you will keep satisfaction at bay. You will find yourself on the mountain of contentment when you decide not to be brainwashed, coerced, purchased, manipulated, or cheated. When you transition into a butterfly, all the caterpillars will try to hold you back, demanding that you remain with them. Remember, you now have wings.

Insensitive memories can smother your development and growth. It can lead you away from authentic contentment. Find the skills and mental capacity to halt the hold of these inhibiting influences from the past. Wake up and recognise the siren song of self-justification. Bring yourself into focus. Only you can persuade yourself to believe privately what you live out publicly. It is a natural response to feel anger over an injury. Permit it, dissect it, and never allow it to simmer. Be strategic even with your setbacks; it will diminish your energy that could be used to improve your life. Festering with your unbridled anger will steer you away from contentment. Dig deep to demonstrate resolve. Sadly, revenge goes hand in glove with anger. Do not deliciously hope for revenge; it drains you of vigour eventually. Contentment will never come in if you continue to allow the injury to constrain your progress.

When a person creates a mental armour of self-justification that can be pierced by indisputable evidence, satisfaction in this arena may be difficult. It creates a national canvas for injustice. It will sweep in sadness and eventually create a huge dent in your level of contentment. There is no doubt that you will have to make such a glaring effort to absolve yourself of culpability. Resentment will spin a tight web around you, oozing out every drop of contentment – life is not curated like a fairy tale, to be fair. Everyone can recognise a hypocrite in action except the hypocrite. It is a mammoth task to use your energy towards your contentment rather than conquering the hypocrite syndrome. Don't blur moral lapses and ignore the discrepancies between actions and moral convictions – use your energy where it matters. Guilt is another emotion that stands between you, your dreams, and your satisfaction in life. Who you once were and who you must befit yet again, despite the circumstances. Forgive your emotions. Embrace life with all that unlocks your heart to the elements that bring you contentment: joy, peace, integrity, and truth. The fiercest aspect of a relationship is with yourself, finding satisfaction with the fragmented pieces. The ache will educate you into who you will never be again.

You never know how hard circumstances have been for another person to make the decisions that they do. Never judge a person when you don't know the complete context. Sometimes you would not even come close to coping with the same set of circumstances. No matter what the situation is, always be content with your default decision. Some predicaments in life are beyond your control, and you will be challenged to decide in a flash – summon your heart to find contentment before you close the chapter. You cannot control what happens in your life, but you can certainly control how you respond to it. Your response reflects your attitude. Perfection is an illusion; grasp that we live in a broken world, and inhumane things happen. You may never understand why it has happened. The abundant living begins when you transcend to the other side and leave behind the offence and the fury and deliberately choose the right outcome for yourself.

Life is an expression that forces an audience to respond. Reinstate your faith and find yourself back to a definition of beauty that finds its source in the perfect character of God – let God direct your path. Even if you have hardly scratched that surface with this approach. It can both reflect your experiences and shape the way you are in your current crisis or the future. Never abandon yourself because you feel you need to conform to the pattern of society. Sometimes we are thrust into situations that have no familiar pattern – the hardest moments to make wise decisions. Sometimes all the pieces shatter, and you will never be able to put them back together again. Life changes in a nanosecond. Find your contentment in this thread; not one of us is guaranteed anything in life. Realise your entire life can change in a New York minute.

We have all gone through seasons where we felt winter was too long. You lost a loved one, a relationship failed, you lost your job, and good friends betrayed you. Develop and learn to take it in your stride and eventually find your equilibrium. It is a different kettle of fish when everything is taken from you without notice. Are you mentally prepared to find your balance in this moment of despair – are you seeking contentment in your final moments on earth? I watched in horror as a documentary captured the final moments of so many lives. People were trapped. The vortex consumed them. They were literally taking their last breaths. Yet they found an avenue to decide to be content with how life ends for them.

"The Falling Man is a photograph taken by Associated Press photographer Richard Drew of a man falling from the World Trade Centre during the September 11 attacks in New York City. The unidentified man in the image was trapped on the upper floors of the North Tower, and it is unclear whether he fell while searching for safety or he jumped to escape the fire and smoke. The photograph was taken at exactly 9:41:15 a.m. on the day of the attacks. The photograph was widely criticized after publication in international media on September 12, 2001, with readers labelling the image as 'disturbing, cold-blooded, ghoulish, and sadistic.' However, in the years following, the photo has gained acclamation. Now regarded as a masterpiece in photojournalism, it is regarded as one of the greatest and most important pieces of art from the 21st century. A Time Magazine retrospective published in 2016 stated, 'Falling Man's identity is still unknown, but he is believed to have been an employee at the Windows on the World restaurant, which sat atop the north tower. The true power of Falling Man, however, is less about who its subject was and more about what he became: a makeshift Unknown Soldier in an often unknown and uncertain war, suspended forever in history.'

Of the 2,606 victims killed inside the World Trade Centre and on the ground in New York City during the September 11 attacks, some have estimated that at least 200 people fell or jumped to their deaths, while other estimates put the number around 100. Almost all these individuals came from the North Tower. Officials could not recover or identify the bodies of those forced out of the buildings prior to the collapse of the towers. The New York City medical examiner's office said it does not classify the people who fell to their deaths on September 11 as 'jumpers,' explaining that a 'jumper' is defined as someone who 'goes to the office in the morning knowing that they will commit suicide,' adding that the victims who fell from the towers did not want to die but were forced out by the smoke and flames or blown out."

Recalling this documentary and the incident still sends chills down my spine. Some family members candidly spoke about their loved ones and their final moments. Either confirming or denying that their loved one would have reached a place of satisfaction to end life on their terms and to take a plunge to death rather than to wait for the unknown. Wisdom does not flow from experience; it only originates from reflecting on the involvement – both personal and others. Regardless of whether you are 20 or 80, the correlation between age and wisdom is zero. Attaining perception and stance does not tie in with your age but rather is about the lessons you have gleaned and the choices you have made that bring you contentment, regardless of the circumstances. Contrary to popular misconception, quitting is for losers. Knowing when to stop, how to change direction, what tact to use, how to leave a toxic situation, mandate more, and choosing how to take your last breath when someone else is pulling the strings, finding peace with your fate, perhaps no one will be content to end life on someone else's terms when thrust into the vortex. Will you choose to react or respond? Infused therein is your satisfaction.

In 2014, I first visited America, New York City, and I made the intrepid journey to the 9/11 Ground Zero memorial. It was just two holes in the ground with water features and names of all those who lost their lives. I was in the company of two friends much younger than me. They could not remember precisely when and why this catastrophe unfolded. After our site visit, we sat down for lunch, and it was the most satisfying meal without really consuming anything. Three lasses sat in wonderment, talking about the history, researching what lurked within our soul, and no, we did not find satisfaction in this tragedy. However, we did find peace that invaded our hearts; we prayed for the victims and their families. We wept and left lighter than we arrived; yes, indeed, contentment came out and drizzled itself on us like a forecast day screaming for a ray of sunshine. This visit to the memorial site is a light that will stay with me forever; it compels me to make better choices. It unleashed something in me that I could never put a price tag on. It is far greater than contentment.

In 2019, I travelled to China. One of the destinations on my bucket list was the visit to Tianmen Mountain Glass Skywalk. It is a coiling dragon cliff skywalk that is a see-through skywalk built in Tianmen Mountain in Zhangjiajie National Park, in the Hunan province. Its name means *'Dragon's*

Spiral,' and it even comes complete with the prank that the glass is cracking as you walk on certain parts. It certainly is not for the faint-hearted! I did have my heart in my hands, and I must admit, it was the most terrifying experience of my life. Self-induced and the terror did not even come close to my near-death experience of having a gun on my head during a robbery in South Africa. You can never confirm how you will respond to terror. Even if planned and calculated during emergency planning, the variables and situations are never the same. I shudder to think what the victims of September 11 felt. You never know how much you consider anything until it is actual or deception and becomes a matter of life and death to you.

It is comfortable to say you believe in a path constructed on a mountain that is 4,982 feet high. Your faith is perhaps in the fact that it was constructed to industry standards. The quality is as robust as the process and the standards adhered to. Hypothetically, if you had to walk on cracked glass that was randomly placed there with no standards in construction, how would you feel then? Exposing yourself to a cliff via a piece of glass as your lifeline, perhaps you first want to ascertain just how much you really trust it? Sometimes you will never have to experience the authentic narration of living a grief so callous, but you can still learn from the observation. Life will or will not put you in a situation where you may have to take a leap of faith because there is no other precipice to trust. When or if you are thrust into this predicament, what will your resolve be? Contentment dwells within you. How you view yourself and how God sees you is where the soul finds nourishment. The greater the harmony between the two, the more concord unfolds, and the more stable your level of contentment becomes – especially in a crisis.

The basic essence of contentment captured so eloquently by Judi:

"Don't prioritise your looks, my friend, as they won't last the journey.
Your sense of humour, though, will only get better with age.
Your intuition will grow and expand like a majestic cloak of wisdom.
Your ability to choose your battles will be fine-tuned to perfection.

Your capacity for stillness, for living in the moment, will blossom.
Your desire to live each moment will transcend all other wants.
Your instinct for knowing what (and who) is worth your time will grow and flourish like ivy on a castle wall.

Don't prioritise your looks, my friend;
they will change forevermore. That pursuit is one of much sadness and disappointment.

Prioritise the uniqueness that makes you, you and the invisible magnet that draws in other like-minded souls to dance in your orbit.
These are the things, which will only get better."
Judi Dench

The secret of success often lies in the ability to consistently unwrap contentment – whether ideas, experiences, or opportunities. This involves a keen awareness of one's surroundings and a willingness to explore beyond the surface. Successful individuals cultivate a mindset of curiosity, breaking down complex concepts into actionable insights. They embrace learning from failures and seek collaboration, transforming challenges into stepping stones. By fostering a habit of reflection and adaptation, they not only reveal the layers of their potential but also inspire others to do the same, creating a dynamic cycle of growth and achievement.

You become content when you stop fighting those who gossip about you.
You become content when you stop warfare with every Tom, Dick, and Harry!

You become content when you stop demanding attention and recognition!
You become content when you stop striving to meet expectations!
You become content when you stop handing the keys to your happiness to inconsiderate people!

You become content when you STOP pleasing everyone!
You become content when you stop the desire to prove others wrong!
Are you CONTENT to let the curtain fall when you have no control?

Use your energy to determine your vision, your dreams, and your destiny. The day that you give up on small fights is the day that you begin to unravel your path to contentment. Some fights are not worth your time. Choose what you fight for wisely. I counted my years and found that I have less time to live from here on than I have lived up to now, so I strategically focus on winning the war, not the battle. I feel like the little girl who won a packet of sweets: she ate the first with pleasure, but when she realised that there were few left; she began to enjoy them intensely. I no longer have time for endless meetings where statutes, rules, procedures, and internal regulations are discussed, knowing that nothing will be achieved. I no longer have time to support the absurd people who, despite their chronological age, have not grown up.

My time is too short. I want the essence of my soul to find contentment. I don't have many sweets in the package anymore, so I am very mindful about time, purpose, and what needs to be accomplished. I want to live next to human people, very human, who know how to laugh at their mistakes, but most importantly, how to use their energy to fix their mistakes. I want to share my table with those who are not inflated by their triumphs. A cohort who will carry their responsibilities to be a beacon of hope and not throw rocks at others who are shining a light for humanity. I want to dance with human dignity as we defend and move towards truth, empathy, and HOPE.

How contentment unravels for me: I want to surround myself with people who know how to touch hearts, people who have been taught by the hard blows of life to grow with gentle touches of the soul and be the difference.

Yes, I'm in a hurry. I'm in a hurry to live with the intensity that only maturity and contentment can give. My goal is to reach the end satisfied. I'm at peace with my loved ones and my conscience. Contentment takes on a deeper significance when you realise that you only have one precious life.

Mateus William's observation, *"We mature with the damage, not with the years,"* highlights the idea that true personal growth and maturity stem from experiences of hardship and adversity rather than the mere passage of time. This perspective suggests that facing and overcoming challenges is what shapes and refines our character. Adversity forces us to confront our limitations, question our assumptions, and develop resilience. When we experience setbacks or trauma, we are compelled to adapt, find new solutions, and cultivate inner strength. This process of navigating through difficulties often leads to profound self-awareness and emotional growth, which are essential components of maturity.

In contrast, simply growing older does not guarantee maturity. Age may bring experience, but it is the quality and intensity of those experiences that truly shape our understanding of ourselves and the world around us. Without facing significant challenges, we may not develop the depth of empathy, wisdom, and strength that come from having navigated through tough times. This idea also resonates with the notion that suffering can foster compassion. Those who have experienced pain and hardship are often more empathetic towards others in similar situations, as they can relate on a deeper level. This shared understanding can create a sense of connection and community, further enriching our personal development. Ultimately, William's quote reminds us that it is through facing life's trials that we gain the most significant insights and growth. Embracing challenges and learning from our *"damage"* enables us to become more resilient, compassionate, and mature individuals.

How content are you with…

- Are you confident in yourself to find your contentment if your life was ending in a few minutes?

- How do you find contentment after a loved one has hurt you?

- How will you attain satisfaction with your unforeseen circumstances that are beyond your control?

Craft the Right Attitude

When I lived in New Zealand, I lived in South Auckland. Commuting to the north side was traversing across the Auckland Bridge – yes, contending with all that traffic. We were looking to purchase a washing machine. My ex-husband found a great deal for a cash purchase, but we had to drive to the north side. I was reluctant to travel all that way. I was happy to pay more just to buy local. My ex-husband contested, saying this is a great deal. We took the plunge. When we arrived at the store on the north side, I was on the phone, so I remained in the car. My ex-husband had already spoken to the salesman via the phone and confirmed that he would be coming into the store to make the purchase. So, he went into the store while I concluded the call and entered the store. My ex-husband was concluding the purchase deal. The salesman was dealing with all the paperwork. I did not interrupt; I occupied myself with aimless browsing.

After a while, the salesman walked up to me and asked if I needed any help. I replied no – I am here with my husband, and we are purchasing a washing machine. My ex-husband walked over. None of us envisaged the din that sallied forth. The salesman was so comfortable speaking out precisely what he thought. *"This is your husband. Why did you marry him? You are like beauty and the beast!"* It is an understatement to say that my ex-husband was not impressed. Our eyes met, and I was speechless with the salesman standing right beside us. My ex-husband broke the silence and exclaimed, *"I will not be purchasing that washing machine. I want a refund."*

Impeccable character...and then some. My ex-husband endeavoured to live by the blueprint of his beliefs, the Bible. Ostensibly, the salesman was acutely aware that we trekked all the way across the bridge to purchase his product. He was confident because the purchase contract was done and dusted. He found satisfaction in addressing his customers with his truth. Without my acquiescence, the purchase was refunded, and we were in the car ready to drive home. I mentioned to my ex-husband that I recalled with fierce clarity that he confirmed to me this was the best deal. *"Don't bother about the sales guy, just take the deal and dismiss him."* I tried to reason.

"It is the best deal, but I am not content with the service," he exclaimed. We were both content to pay more and not be treated unprofessionally. Never forget that you always have a choice, even when you are presented with the best deal. Satisfaction goes deeper than just monetary saving. You must live with that choice and let it sit well with you. Your contentment is hemmed into the fabric of the calibre of service received, personality traits, emotions, philosophies, and moods only if you allow it. You can let the buck stop with you. Often unconsciously, your mind is seeking a pattern, symmetry, order, and expressions that will speak to you of meaning, of your values, aligning you to be at peace with the situation or flee in the opposite direction. Pay

attention to your intuition; it will pave a path to contentment.

"Our plans miscarry because they have no aim. When a man does not know what harbour, he is making for, no wind is the right wind." – Seneca. Even when someone takes the liberty to test your worth, rest assured in your own confidence of knowing who you are. When you let others describe who you are, then contentment will never be your portion. Understand and live like you know that no one can trigger you, instigate you or question your worth, force you around, or bully you. Do not permit anyone to allow you to lose your self-worth.

Allure is exposed in nature, music, art, pictures, and so much more; however, the most attractive is the character of a human. It gives new meaning to beauty and human experience when you have the tact to control your tongue and add colour to the inventory of someone else's life. Contentment will find you when you choose not to create apprehension in hearts. Your actions and words correspond to the tangible aspects of human experience. If there is a shape or trajectory to the experience of hurt in a broken heart, or the experience of awe, what do you think will satisfy both parties and invite contentment in? Conforming to situations just to keep the peace is a trauma response. When you do this, you are disrespecting your own boundaries. Refrain from making yourself uncomfortable for others to feel comfortable. Gain control of your life and use your actions and voice to be seen, heard, and content. Always speak with kindness and consideration for the other person.

When we were young adults, my friend – her nom de plume in this book is Suraya, and I loved watching Bollywood movies. Post movie, we would always have a philosophical discussion. Suraya frequently mentioned how she would love to be an Indian wife – proudly wearing Sindhoor and bindi. *Sindooram is a traditional vermilion red or orange-red coloured cosmetic powder from the Indian subcontinent, usually worn by married women along the part of their hairline. In Hindu communities, the Sindhoor is a visual marker of the marital status of a woman, and ceasing to wear it usually implies widowhood. The bindi is a bright dot of some colour applied in the centre of the forehead that symbolises marriage. In modern times, unmarried women wear colourful stick-on dots as a fashion tradition.*

A dream of a traditional wedding monopolised many hours of her time. Haldi is known to purify and cleanse the body of the couple entering holy matrimony. It also marks an auspicious beginning of a new life together. Haldi is believed to protect the bride and the groom from any bad omen that might harm them before the big day. Both the bride and groom have a turmeric, a.k.a. haldi ceremony the day before the wedding. The bride also has a henna ceremony, which is a distinct act of becoming a bride. All this tradition created an extra layer of emotions in Suraya and her future wedding.

With the progression of more than three decades, Suraya's life did not pan out like the dreams she envisioned. She tersely fell in love with no glorious conclusion ever in sight. Rakesh promised her all the lip service but was so short on action. He was married with kids, and he promised to leave them but never acted on it, even after Suraya had a child with him. She longed for her fairytale wedding and to marry only Rakesh. Suraya spent almost 30 years waiting for the man she loved to propose, and he never did. Suraya was never content with the circumstances, but I watched her reconcile with it. She was stuck between a rock and a hard place. She protracted as a Hindu bride: she wore the bindi and mangalsutra. Yet contentment eluded her.

Life was traced and erratic for Suraya; she wondered why Rakesh promised her the world but delivered nothing, yet she continued to wait three decades to find contentment from a person. One day Suraya had an epiphany that the prime of her life had passed her by and only she could find satisfaction with where life was at. Fundamentally, it dawned on her that the rest of her life could be the best of her life if she lived it authentically content. Rakesh was not averse to a little dalliance with a desperate want-to-be housewife. This was how he enslaved Suraya like a puppet on a string.

Quagmire does not guarantee marriage; realise this. Illness does not denote death. Wealth is not the definition of prosperity. Obtaining a plush house is not possessing comfort or concord. Driving a swanky car does not guarantee you will reach your destination. Throwing on the finest apparel threads does not mean you will be the prettiest in the room. Education is not the hallmark for wisdom. Winning an argument does not correlate to victory. There is so much to conquer before you reach the castle of contentment. People will promise you the world to keep you in the web. The onus is upon you to map out your boundaries and exactly what you need for your life to be content. Never hand the keys to another person. Don't be delusional about the virtuous elements in people; search for the genuine instead and realise that the talker is often dressed in false clothing, the doer is transparent and delivers on every promise no matter what the battle scars are.

You will never find contentment with a person who strings you along with lip service. Honest living begins with action. Realise that you are a non-duplicated miracle and never bind your life or worth to another person who cannot respect or honour you. If you are in a maelstrom, I beseech you to find yourself. Unravel all the extra layers of emotions. Purpose to be still. Scripture says a man plans, but God directs. Allow God to direct your path. Unravel what personal contentment means to you. To be an astonishing character, a great mother, an authentic wife, a distinct daughter, a noticeable friend, and an impeccable professional, you must first find yourself. Look in the mirror and have real conversations; proactively discover your blind spots. You cannot fill other people's cups if your own is empty. Forgive what you cannot forget and watch the dial spin to satisfaction.

Never search for happiness in others; it will lead you to a path of loneliness.

Resolve to make the laconic mode your default character. God will enlarge you despite those that betrayed you. Never wear that distant expression frequently and glide into autopilot mode. Live with purpose and constantly self-introspect yourself. Realign with crucial changes and don't spend your life picking stones while you lose sight of the actual gem. Contentment will come to those who have conquered the ostrich syndrome. Contentment is being happy with who you are, with the people in your life, and with the state of your life. It is a habit of respect for your reality. Admiration for who you are just as you are and reverence for others just as they are. When you are content, this moment is more than sufficient; the simple pleasure will keep you well pleased.

We all have an ideal of what life should look like. When one veers off the path, then some may shun you. Suraya's life did not pan out as she envisaged, but she found her rendition of love with deficiencies that felt real. Only you get to define and settle on a path in life. You either feel clear-minded and undisturbed, thus very excited about life, or you feel vulnerable, nervous, or resentful and annoyed with the outcome of your life. Whichever path life has you on, remember that your life experience is speaking to you; deep within, only you understand if you are content with the state of play or not. Everyone experiences challenges in their lives. No one is 100% happy – everyone is dealing with something. No matter what life unravels to you, you need to journey back to your authentic self and introspect if you are satisfied on the path that life has placed you on. Every experience creates the potential for growth and improvement. The most challenging form of experiences ignites from the condition of your mind and your self-talk. Discern if you are indulging in negative or positive self-talk. Your contentment level will correlate with your level of transformation.

Finding contentment in the most treacherous circumstances, especially when those we nurture and trust cause us pain, requires profound resilience and inner strength. In such moments, it's crucial to shift focus from the hurt to the lessons learned, acknowledging that love can sometimes lead to heartache. Practicing self-compassion is essential; allowing oneself to feel the pain while also recognising the courage it takes to continue nurturing, both for oneself and for others. Seeking solace in supportive relationships and community can provide the comfort and validation needed to heal. Engaging in mindfulness and gratitude practices can help cultivate a sense of peace, even amidst turmoil. Ultimately, digging deep for contentment means embracing the complexity of love and pain, finding meaning in the struggles, and fostering hope for brighter days ahead.

Search Within

Never miscalculate a cycle breaker; when you stand in the face of an ordeal and contest to the end, it is courageous and influential. It outweighs any significant cost when you are a cycle breaker. Things can be restored. Not with time, as the cliché goes, but with intention. Go forward deliberately, extravagantly, and categorically. The fragmented world awaits in obscurity for you to lustre the light that is within you. Accomplishment is not just about what you accomplish in your life; it's about what you inspire others to do. Make your relations transformational, not just transactional. Understand the fundamental difference between the intention and the excuse. Consent with no excuses and perform with reason. Be unapologetically tenacious and invest in what matters.

The reality exists not so much for the purpose of making things up, but for acknowledging correlation, relation between things – seeing connections. It is not by accident that we agree that the rhythm discovered in a brisk walk to the podium reflects confidence, or urgency, while a broken rhythm implies uncertainty, commotion, and apprehension. We have experienced the connection between these things so often that we have learned to become fluent in this language. We look for correlation in everyday life, yet we ignore so much that is glaring at us. Some of us have mastered the art of looking for correlation only in certain places. We are content to turn a blind eye when satisfaction is lacking in a colossal form and leads to destruction. How are we inheritors of finite wisdom? Are you content to live in this mode?

One evening I was flicking through the channels on the television – a documentary soon stole my attention: *"Kaavan, a male Asian elephant known as the 'world's loneliest elephant' after his partner Saheli died in 2012. Kaavan was gifted by the government of Sri Lanka to Pakistan in 1985. He remained at the Islamabad Zoo until November 2020, when he was moved to a sanctuary in Cambodia in response to a campaign launched by local and international animal rights activists led by American singer Cher. An American veterinarian, Samar Khan, visited Islamabad Zoo in 2015 and was disturbed by Kaavan's condition and environment. She started a petition on Change.org to plead for Kaavan's release to an elephant sanctuary. Khan's petition received more than 400,000 signatures and caught the attention of American singer Cher.*

In response to the petition, zoo officials took some steps to improve Kaavan's care, such as providing additional water and removing his chains. Safwan Shahab Ahmad, the vice-chairman of the Pakistan Wildlife Foundation, identified some of Kaavan's behaviour as a kind of mental illness, possibly connected to the conditions in which he was kept. In September 2017, a news report highlighted the dire condition in which Kaavan was living, including being bound in chains for over two decades. A second petition requesting Kaavan's release gathered more than 200,000 signatures. Owais Awan, a Pakistani lawyer, sued the Islamabad Zoo to demand Kaavan's release.

On 21 May 2020, the Islamabad High Court ruled that Kaavan should be freed, and the zoo closed. It ordered wildlife officials to consult with Sri Lankan authorities to find a suitable sanctuary for Kaavan in another country within thirty days. The court also criticised the zoo officials for failing to meet the animal's needs in terms of the violation of the Prevention of Cruelty to Animals Act 1890 and Wildlife Ordinance of 1979."

I had so many questions. This elephant was a gift to the prime minister's daughter. Did they not feel a need to have some duty of care and welfare? Right at the top of the pecking order and very satisfied with the situation for almost three decades. Is this a classic case of I hate the gift you got me, so I tossed it out? What's astounding is that the partner, Saheli, died in 2012 due to constant tugging of a chain on the foot – literally a torn foot! Yet the zoo kept Kavaan chained by his foot. Kavaan was in mental anguish, and people still called into the zoo to watch him for entertainment. For thirty years everyone seemed content with the situation. Even the zookeepers could not decipher what animal satisfaction was, and the legal pundits of the land cared not to look at the injustice – a country that had legislation to prevent cruelty to animals but no real clout to enforce it.

Do you find contentment in neglect? If you cannot care for an animal, how can you be trusted with humans? Eclectic characters fill our world; some are decidedly dilapidated in virtue. Are you living an unapologetic life? Are you content to be a leader, entrusted to uphold the law, or simply be a human who has a moral compass? When you make choices that align with both your welfare and the welfare of animals, you can put your head on the pillow, feeling a sense of satisfaction. Some hearts bleed enough for all those who do not care. The veterinarian, Samar Khan, and singer Cher are replicas of what empathy is like in action. Cher commented, *'It was better than a night at the Oscars… an experience like no other experience.'* Gratification at its best helping an animal who can do nothing for you in return. Empathy is often an unheeded skill in negotiation. Approaching arbitration with a two-way attitude will lead you to an outcome that pleases both parties – even if the other party is just an animal. You cannot find peace when you deliberately induce pain and suffering into any equation.

People are not born strong. People cultivate durability, from small to big things, by absolving not to run from the situation but to allow it to grow in new ways. Especially when this approach will cost you dearly – the life lesson will pay dividends. *"The only impossible journey is the one you never begin."* – Tony Robbins. The courage it takes to do what's noble is the courage that lives within you. We all have options when we make choices. You cannot persuade a heart to care no more than you could convince a fire to cool down. Evidently the choice is always living in the abundance of your heart. Karma is not going to arrive in a jiffy and fix the plight here and now. Transcend by improving your critical thinking and enhancing your mindset. The world will never get over the trauma that you create; they are simply compelled to learn to live with it while some may step in to help the victims blossom despite it. Introduction to satisfaction despite a flawed agenda! Before you taint the world with your actions, ask yourself if your action is necessary and does it improve the drama?

"The average American carries out five good deeds a month, according to a survey.

The Top 10 Good Deeds
Helped someone with directions: 66%.

Held the door open for a stranger: 65%.

Let someone with fewer items go in front of me in line at a store: 60%.

Helped someone cross the street: 60%.

Completed a chore/errand for a family member or friend: 56%.

Gave a dollar or so to charity when checking out while shopping: 56%.

Donated clothes to a thrift store: 55%.

Helped someone carry their groceries home: 55%.

Returned a lost item that I found: 55%.

Paid for a stranger's meal: 53%.

Top Charities People Prefer Donating To

Charities that help children: 76%.

Charities that help women: 61%.

Charities that help the environment: 56%.

Charities that help animals: 38%.

The nicest things strangers have done for people:

- *A stranger once gave me a change of clothes and some tea and let me use their shower after I was caught outside in a severe storm in Florida on a business trip.*

- *I am an older person and should not be doing some of the things I do. Last winter, a neighbour's boyfriend helped me shovel my driveway.*

- *I had nowhere to go and no money, and a stranger gave me a ride to the closest hotel, paid for my stay, bought me a hot meal, took me back to my room, and left me with about a hundred dollars.*

- *My car got hit by a drunk driver and took off. A man who witnessed it stayed with me until the police arrived to give his account.*

- *An employee at a Walmart store approached my son, who was throwing a huge tantrum, and offered him a snack to calm him down.*

- *I was driving back from the ER in the middle of the night with my toddler when I got a flat tire. I pulled over to the side, but it was at a very quiet and dark part of the interstate. A big rig truck pulled over, told me to sit in his cab to keep warm, and he would change my tire."*

I cannot find a survey conducted in Pakistan; it would be astonishing to view how much this nation gives, especially to the welfare of animals. In my book, *Don't Just Fly, SOAR:* "Low levels of oxytocin in the brain are associated with several mental health conditions, including depression, anxiety, social phobia, post-traumatic stress disorder, etc. Research suggests that if you increase oxytocin, it can lead to the following benefits: reduce stress and anxiety, increase feeding calmness and security, improve mood, and increase feelings of contentment. The list goes on.

Oxytocin evidently does a lot. Due to this, some doctors have started prescribing oxytocin to their patients to help treat their mental health symptoms. However, you don't necessarily need to rush to your doctor to obtain a prescription. You can practice natural ways to increase oxytocin in the brain. There are several avenues to explore; I will let you conduct your own research. Nonetheless, I will just share one profound effect that impacts a dramatic sphere: 'Give someone a gift or simply be a blessing.' Studies show that receiving and giving gifts or blessings increases oxytocin levels in the brain. So, imagine the ripple effect this has on society when you increase someone's oxytocin level, and they are elated with positive vibes, and they pay the prescription forward. A natural prescription with no side effects."

In my book, *Making Sage Decisions*, I wrote about the dramatic effect of animal welfare that caught my eye in South Africa. I have included the excerpt from my book: *"During one of my sojourns to South Africa, I attended a family wedding. I was amazed to hear revision in the generic marriage vows that echoed from the priest. A few years later, I had another invitation to attend another wedding in South Africa. I have attended a substantial number of weddings in this neck of the woods. What brought on the change in vows? Not sure, but my hat goes out to them for making this decision. Globally, the majority (57%) of consumers own pets. This statistic is sadly coupled with unfortunate abuse of pets. I was astounded and relieved to hear the Hindu marriage vows enhanced to include care for pets. Yes indeed, someone in their finite wisdom made the sage decision to include this detail in marriage nuptials.*

*In Australia the domestic violence clause for restraining parties also includes these details to protect a person **and their pets**. People are waking up to cold and brutal behaviour towards animals, but we still seem to prevail with humans. Life is not always intrinsically pleasurable, but we can carve a better tomorrow with innovation and more significant decisions. What a breath of fresh air to note these fundamental changes in society. The complex constellation of responses is only worthy by the choices that underpin it. In what ways, shape, and form do you volunteer a morsel of unsentimental wisdom? Are you the paragon of sound judgement and rationale?"*

The universe giving you a clerical error is a vivid sign. Take heed if you value contentment. Tame all your unpleasant brew that generates distress and phobias. Don't just move the bad memories into the attic of your mind. Understand the impact and importance of dealing with the root cause. Your actions will pay dividends. Do you understand the difference between success and significance? Success often emphasises external achievements, such as wealth, status, or recognition, while significance centres on the impact one has on others and the broader world. Success can lead to temporary satisfaction, but it may not always provide deep contentment. In contrast, significance fosters a sense of purpose and fulfillment, as it aligns with personal values and contributes to the well-being of others. Ultimately, true contentment arises when individuals find a balance between success and significance, prioritising meaningful contributions over mere accolades, leading to a richer, more rewarding life experience.

In the final hours of life, a cancer patient may find contentment not in the absence of pain but in the profound acceptance of their journey and the connections they have nurtured along the way. This deep sense of peace arises from a heart filled with gratitude for the love shared, the lessons learned, and the moments cherished. Despite their circumstances, they embody remarkable resilience, offering wisdom and support to those around them, transforming their experience into a source of inspiration. This illustrates that contentment is not merely a destination reserved for the end; it is a state of being we should strive for from the very beginning. By cultivating gratitude, connection, and compassion throughout our lives, we can embrace joy and meaning at every stage, turning even the darkest moments into opportunities for growth and love. Never stagnate in your setback, and do not wait to be on your deathbed to contemplate contentment. Nourish your soul daily.

How content are you with...

- Do you allow other people to walk all over you and then sulk over it?

- Do you establish healthy boundaries even if it costs you?

- Describe your default mood in life: do you feel down, do you feel overwhelmed, or do you feel confident and satisfied?

- Do you feel content when you dish out pain and suffering to others?

The Correlation Between Happiness and Contentment

Happiness is not attained. It is in your mind. Get your mindset aligned, and your attitude and vibe will follow. *"We cannot cure the world of sorrows, but we can choose to live in joy."* – Joseph Campbell. Is happiness an illusion? Happiness is strongly affiliated with contentment. Why? Can you be content even when you are unhappy? When most people seek happiness, they pursue pleasure: great food, more money, more materialism, looking better, and, sadly, obtaining more likes on social media. Pleasure is correlated with happiness but does not cause it. Inquire of any random sex chaser how their pursuit of pleasure turned out. Probe a husband who had an affair, shattered his wife's heart, and tore the dreams of his children. Ask the teenager who ate himself to health conditions how his pleasure ultimately made him feel. Research indicates that people who focus their energy on materialistic and superficial pleasures end up more apprehensive, more emotionally unbalanced, and less happy in the long run. Pleasure is the most superficial form of life satisfaction and, therefore, the simplest. Pleasure is what's marketed to us. Happiness is understanding what brings personal joy, and contentment is being satisfied in any given circumstances.

PLEASURE ≠ HAPPINESS ≠ CONTENTMENT

"What Is Cherophobia in Psychology? The term cherophobia, originating from the Greek term 'chairo,' which means 'to rejoice,' is the aversion to or fear of happiness. While cherophobia is not currently recognized as a clinical disorder under the Diagnostic and Statistical Manual of Mental Disorders (DSM-5), several studies have begun to validate its existence scientifically (Joshanloo, 2014). What is happiness? To effectively understand its underpinnings, happiness first needs to be defined. In psychological research, 'happiness' is often used interchangeably with the term 'subjective wellbeing' and measured by asking individuals to report on their life satisfaction and the presence or absence of positive and negative affect (Diener, Suh, Lucas, & Smith, 1999). While there's still no conclusive consensus, a widely accepted definition of happiness was proposed by the positive psychology researcher Sonja Lyubomirsky in her book The How of Happiness (2007). She described happiness as: 'The experience of joy, contentment, or positive well-being, combined with a sense that one's life is good, meaningful, and worthwhile.' This definition incorporates the transient feelings that individuals experience, such as elation, pride, gratitude, and contentment, brought about by a deeper fulfillment with a good life."

Would you rather be happy or content? What continues to vex society still is having one without the other, and it will forever remain an enigma, but yes, indeed, it is possible to be content even in the presence of calamities. Any deviation from the mindset may be met with swift shunning. Tread the slow path back to satisfaction, even if it's a lion's heart wrapped in a buck's hide. Happiness is essentially different from an emotion. Adequately, it is an experience typically hallmarked by optimistic rationality, joyfulness, satisfaction, and even amusement. Contentment is a lingering feeling supplemented by tranquillity, appreciation, and gratification. Happiness is a short-term feeling, whereas contentment holds the capacity to last indefinitely. Why do so many pursue happiness rather than contentment? If you conduct an online search for *'how to be happy'* on your search engine, it will return more than seven billion results in less than one second. However, if you search the keywords *'how to be content,'* the results returned reflect a little more than 18 million results. Evidently, this indicates society's desire for a happiness high – the euphoria that comes with enjoyment and pleasure. This experiment plainly validates a lack of interest in the approach to chase peacemaking and satisfaction, albeit longer-lasting, expression of contentment.

Statistics of People Who Report They Are Happy

In recent years, global studies on happiness have revealed intriguing patterns, particularly when comparing pre and post COVID-19 data. According to the 2023 World Happiness Report, while 57% of people worldwide reported being happy in 2019, that figure dropped to 52% by 2021. The COVID-19 pandemic, with its widespread isolation, health concerns, and economic instability, had a noticeable impact on people's sense of well-being. However, even as the pandemic receded, global happiness levels showed a slow but steady rebound, with reports indicating a slight improvement by 2023, although still not back to pre-pandemic levels. Interestingly, happiness correlates strongly with factors such as social support, income, and life expectancy, but post COVID-19, the emphasis has shifted towards mental health, work-life balance, and a deeper appreciation for community and personal connections. This shift highlights how the pandemic not only altered day-to-day living but also reshaped how people measure and define contentment.

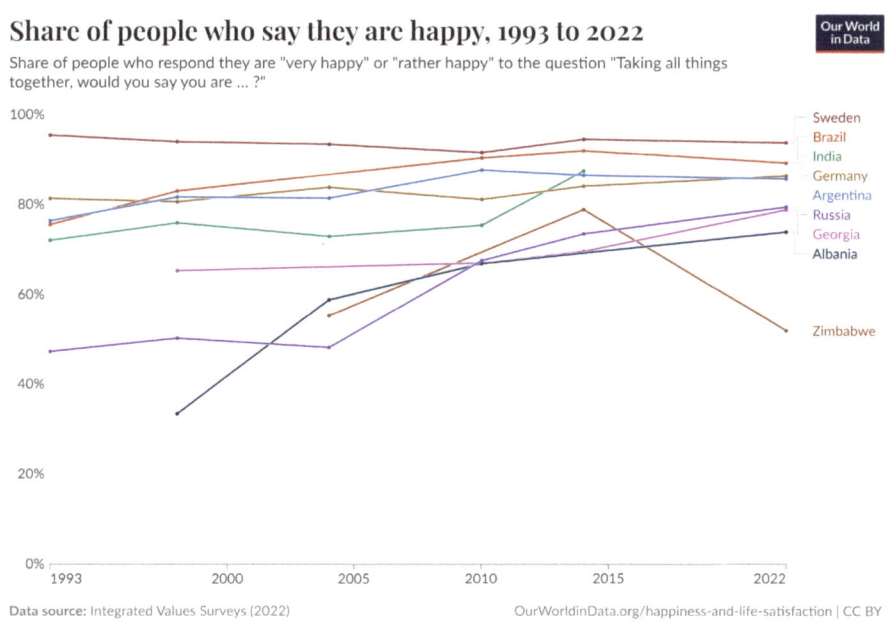

Graph: People Who Say They Are Happy

As we can see, in most countries, the trend is positive: In most countries with data from two or more surveys, the most recent observation is higher than the earliest. In some cases, the improvement has been very large; in Albania, for example, the share of people who reported being 'very happy' or 'rather happy' went from 33.4% in 1998 to 73.9% in 2022.

The Distribution of Life Satisfaction
In examining the global distribution of life satisfaction, it becomes clear that contentment is a deeply nuanced and culturally dependent concept. According to self-reported life satisfaction data, regions such as Scandinavia and parts of Western Europe consistently rank higher, with individuals reporting greater overall life satisfaction. In contrast, many regions in Sub-Saharan Africa and parts of Southeast Asia show lower averages, reflecting not just economic disparities but varying societal values and expectations. Global surveys, including the World Happiness Report, reveal that while economic stability, health, and freedom of choice are significant contributors to life satisfaction, cultural factors – such as community, family, and spiritual beliefs – shape how contentment is perceived and prioritized. What contentment means to people around the world is therefore not universal, but rather a spectrum that shifts with local priorities and historical contexts. In this light, contentment isn't merely a static state of happiness or fulfillment but a dynamic interplay of personal and collective factors that vary as much as the people who experience it.

Most of the studies comparing happiness and life satisfaction among countries focus on averages. However, distributional differences are also important.

Life satisfaction is often reported on a scale from 0 to 10, with 10 representing the highest possible level of satisfaction. This is the so-called 'Cantril Ladder'. This visualization shows how responses are distributed across steps in this ladder. In each case, the height of the bars is proportional to the fraction of answers at each score. Each differently coloured distribution refers to a world region, and for each region, we have overlaid the distribution for the entire world as a reference.

These plots show that in Sub-Saharan Africa – the region with the lowest average scores – the distributions are consistently to the left of those in Europe.

This means that the share of people who are 'happy' is lower in Sub-Saharan Africa than in Western Europe, independently of which score in the ladder we use as a threshold to define 'happy'. Similar comparisons can be made by contrasting other regions with high average scores (e.g., North America, Australia, and New Zealand) against those with low average scores (e.g., South Asia).

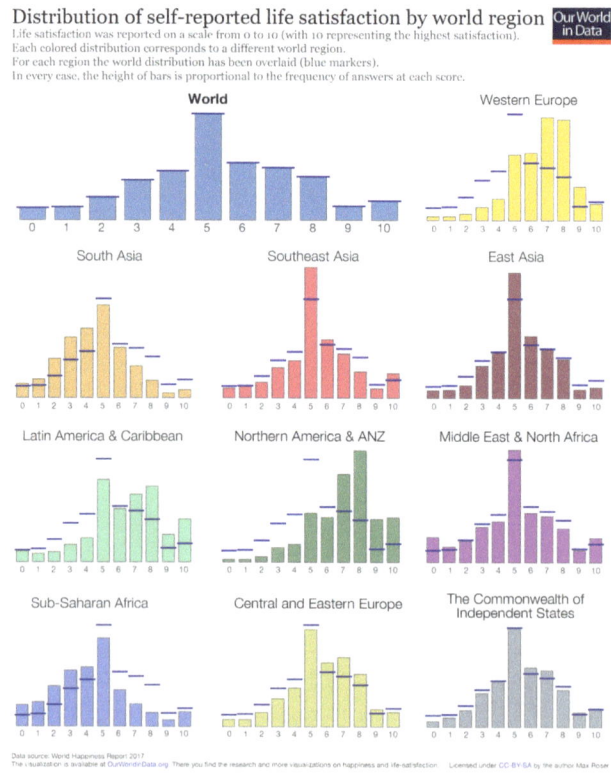

Graph: Self Reported Life Satisfaction

"The happiness of your life depends upon the quality of your thoughts. Guard accordingly and take care that you entertain no notions unsuitable to virtue and reasonable nature." – Marcus Aurelius.

Happiness is fading experiences; contentment is an attitude that you cultivate to carry you in every season of life. External factors influence happiness, whereas contentment is influenced by both external and internal factors. Happiness is on a short-term basis, whereas contentment is more long-term. Happiness is an emotion, but contentment is an attitude and state of mind. Happiness is a reaction, whereas contentment is a lasting calmness that stays with you. Life challenges will teach you, and eventually, you glean how to practice contentment.

You cannot wake up tomorrow and be content. It takes determination, self-awareness, and commitment. Satisfaction takes time and calls you to look within, and contentment is worth every iota of effort you put in.

Happiness and contentment are often used interchangeably, yet they represent distinct states of being that influence our overall well-being. Understanding their differences is crucial for achieving a more profound sense of fulfilment in life.

Happiness: The Fleeting Emotion

Happiness is typically associated with short-term feelings of joy or pleasure. It often arises from external circumstances – achievements, relationships, or experiences. For instance, receiving a promotion at work, enjoying a fun outing with friends, or indulging in a favourite meal can evoke happiness. However, this happiness is often fleeting; it fades as the excitement diminishes or as life presents new challenges. This transient nature of happiness can lead individuals to constantly chase the next source of joy, creating a cycle of highs and lows.

Contentment: A Deeper State of Being

In contrast, contentment represents a more profound and enduring state of satisfaction. It emerges from within and is less dependent on external factors. Contentment arises when individuals accept their current situation and appreciate what they have rather than fixating on what they lack. This acceptance fosters a sense of peace, allowing one to find joy in everyday moments and simple pleasures. Unlike happiness, which may come and go, contentment can provide a steady foundation for emotional resilience.

The Correlation Between Happiness and Contentment

While happiness can contribute to a sense of contentment, it is not a prerequisite for it. Many people experience periods of unhappiness – such as loss, disappointment, or hardship – yet can still feel contentment by recognising the value of their experiences and maintaining a perspective of gratitude. Conversely, an unrelenting pursuit of happiness can lead to frustration and dissatisfaction when expectations are not met.

You are the chief happiness this world affords. Happiness is a mindset, a conscious choice we make every day. It is not about having a perfect life but about finding joy in the little things, cultivating gratitude, and focusing on the positives, even in challenging times. While circumstances can influence our mood, true contentment comes from within – it's an attitude that allows us to see the beauty in imperfections and appreciate what we have rather than what we lack. By choosing to embrace a mindset of contentment, we empower ourselves to live more fulfilling lives, regardless of the ups and downs that come our way. Contentment is not something to chase; it's something to create from the inside out.

Reflections on Happiness
As I navigate through my sixth decade, I often ponder the correlation between happiness and contentment. Happiness is fleeting, tied to moments of success or joy, while contentment is a deeper, more abiding state of being. I realised that true contentment allows happiness to arise organically, enriching my life without dependence on external validation.

In my current phase of life, I find joy not just in significant milestones but in the mundane cooking a meal for loved ones, tending to a garden, or enjoying a quiet evening with a good book. These moments, often overlooked, are where contentment resides, and through them, happiness finds its way back into my life, and contentment overflows.

A Legacy of Contentment
As I look ahead, I hope to impart these lessons to my readers. I want them to understand that while life's journey may lead them far from home, the essence of contentment lies within. It is a mindset cultivated through gratitude, community, acceptance, and resilience. My hope is that they carry these values forward, finding joy not only in achievements but also in the rich tapestry of everyday life.

The decades of my life as an immigrant have been a journey of profound transformation. From the pain of separation to the beauty of connection, I have learned that contentment is a choice – one that allows happiness to flourish in even the most challenging of circumstances. My journey continues, and with each step, I embrace the lessons that life unfolds, knowing that true contentment is a gift I can carry with me wherever I go.

The foundation of contentment lies in a combination of gratitude, acceptance, and self-awareness. Gratitude helps shift focus from what we lack to appreciating what we have, fostering a positive mindset. Acceptance involves embracing our circumstances, recognizing that life is filled with ups and downs, and finding peace in the present moment. Self-awareness allows us to understand our values, desires, and emotional responses, helping us align our choices with what truly matters to us. Together, these elements create a stable base for genuine contentment, enabling us to navigate life's challenges with resilience and grace.

How content are you with...

- Do you define yourself as happy? Why?

- Do you see yourself as content?

- What would you like to improve or implement in your contentment journey?

- Are you content about where your life is heading? If not, how can you change it?

The Benefits of Contentment

Hope can be very difficult, specifically after disillusionment. However, it's a choice. Permit yourself to live after you are hurt. To still attain your dreams and seek contentment in things that bring pleasure to your heart despite the overwhelming pain. You do not have to sacrifice your emotions of grief to warrant your dreams. Perhaps it is the ultimate oxymoron of life – to rise to the challenge amidst impediments. Authenticity is flawless. Discover the foundation of choice. You shape the contours of the outcome far more than you perceive. Live an authentic life – respect your own necessities and embrace your essence, even if you feel you are not worthy in this season or any season to put your needs first. You cannot stop certain things, but you can survive them; you can thrive despite them. Activate your relational intelligence and analyse the circumstances effectively, then step forward to live triumphantly.

Decades from now it will not matter what your emotions felt like on the day. What will go down in history is the choice you made to trudge forward despite the pain. Remember that huge battles are won by daily tasks done every day. The greatest asset in the world is having peace – contentment. You need to decide to navigate through your uncertainties, self-esteem, pain, and gloomy feelings. Regardless of whether you shine or struggle, you need to make choices that will keep you going forward. When you lose a loved one, it is an ever-evolving story in your life. You can never go back to the way things used to be. You must learn how to adapt, how to live with the void, and how to conquer your dreams still.

"In August 1596, William Shakespeare's only son, Hamnet, died in Stratford. He was 11 years old. It was a terrible blow to the playwright. There is a passage in a play, King John, written soon after Hamnet's death, that might give some clues as to Shakespeare's emotional state at the time. The lines are delivered by Constance, the mother of a small boy who has died:

> *Grief fills the room up of my absent child,*
> *Lies in his bed, walks up and down with me,*
> *Puts on his pretty looks, repeats his words,*
> *Remembers me of all his gracious parts,*
> *Stuffs out his vacant garments with his form.*

There is something in those lines that suggests real grief rather than a stagey show of tears. Earlier, she says, 'That we shall see and know our friends in heaven: If that be true, I shall see my boy again.' They are sad lines, and scholars have long sensed something of Shakespeare's loss in them. Fathers and sons figure prominently in several plays that followed Hamnet's death. **Henry IV, part 1 and part 2,** are primarily concerned with the relationship between the King and his tearaway son Hal. **Hamlet**, whose *name is oddly like Shakespeare's son, deals with the child's responsibility to a dead father. There is also **Twelfth Night**, which features twins. One of the twins is thought to be dead but returns. Shakespeare wrote to please his audiences; the idea of the self-conscious writer who talks about himself in every work is a modern one.*

However, there are patterns in the plays that do seem to match some of what is known about Shakespeare's life. The loss of an only son, particularly when his wife Anne was past the age where she could have more children, would have been devastating to a man who seems to have been committed to becoming a gentleman."

Detach from memories that no longer serve you and lead you to contentment. Refrain from isolating each experience and permitting it to derail your dreams. Yes, indeed, the absence of your loved ones does affect the disposition of life, but never let it distort your future. Imagine what our world would be like if William Shakespeare allowed his grief to dictate his future. Realisation and determination yield a brighter future and a healthier tomorrow. Emotions must be acknowledged before they can be structured and channelled. Peace does not denote the absence of toil, misfortune, or difficult work. It means to be present during those things and still compose your heart and channel your energy. When life gets difficult, don't hope for it to get easier. Resolve to be tougher. Shakespeare simulates intense success despite his circumstances, and his work still stands the test of time as the guru of all time in literature.

After trauma, you most definitely will be different; the same synchronisation to your soul no longer exists. You cannot ignore that reality. However, you cannot allow it to chop up the rest of you. You need to relearn how to live and navigate through life without your loved one. You need to find the zeal, obligation, buoyancy, mechanism, and confrontation to strive towards a new canvas of satisfaction. You need to understand that change is the only constant – expect change to unravel in your life and never be afraid of it. When setbacks present, reflect and learn, then take a step forward. Glean the art of separating your distractions; otherwise, your disruptions will separate you from your goals and eventually steal your contentment. Healing yourself is challenging, but the benefits are worth their weight in gold. Actions prove who you are, circumstances unravel your grit, and resolve determines your level of contentment. The greatest humans are those fragmented souls that don't permit discomfort to derail them. Instead, they channel their setbacks to encourage others. Pain makes you tougher; tears generate courage, and heartache fosters wisdom. Be grateful that the experience is mapping out a richer future.

Life is a constant transition – have you accepted that? Few pleasures in life feel more decadent than throwing on the finest threads and looking your best. Do you live like an astute propagandist? Do you know what your non-negotiables are in life? Do you live a life that is aligned with your values, or do you allow society to stymie you? Contentment is the result of reserving the right to process life as it is and how it best aligns with your values rather than conforming to the stereotypes that are enforced upon you. The most attractive asset is authenticity – live a life that is true to yourself. The signal of your character is what you say no to and how that harmonises your parallel to satisfaction. Never assassinate any facet of your character or values to acquire peace – it will not be real.

Wake up your genius and escalate to the tests that are most significant to you. Stimulate yourself as you encourage the world. Relish the facts that you are creative, confident, and a way maker. When you practise your key values despite the discomfort, you will become invigorated. The experience will offer you composure, offering you motivation and a focused mind. You can control many facets of your life, which directly correlates to your contentment. You can control your perspective, how honest you are, what risks you choose to take, what values you live by how much time you waste on worrying, and how often you allow circumstances to drive you. Based on the actuarial data that is mentioned in the previous chapter, we all do have choices, and those choices most definitely affect our contentment tank. It is time to enhance your parochial horizon. Books, minds, and umbrellas only work when they are opened.

"Having made the choice to age gracefully, Sarah Jessica Parker faced condemnation for not conforming to modern beauty ideals and standards, including getting Botox injections and large lips.

As if that was not enough, things turned nasty when the paparazzi released photos of Parker having lunch with 'Bravo' bigwig Andy Cohen. Parker had a make-up-free face with her greying hair on full display, which attracted mean comments. She was shamed of her grey hair and was called old. Andy Cohen, who also has a head of grey hair, came to Parker's defence, wondering why he never received criticism for the same and called the comments 'misogynistic.' 'It almost feels as if people don't want us to be perfectly OK with where we are, as if they almost enjoy us being pained by who we are today, whether we choose to age naturally and not look perfect, or whether you do something that makes you feel better,' Parker hit back at her critics. For many people, this may be the reason to think about their attitude toward aging because it is a natural process and everyone's choice of how they want to look."

Without a shadow of a doubt, Sarah Jessica Parker is content in her own skin and head of grey hair. She is confident about who she is and how she prefers to age. Yet society makes the decision to bully her about her personal boundaries. So much can be revealed by reactions. The abundance of your heart can show exactly how you feel, especially when your approvals are garnished with jealousy. Your conditional support is drenched in envy. Your hate can hide in the bubbles of love. This creates a vortex to live in, with so many facades bombarding your daily life. It will cause you to question most things and misplace your basic satisfaction. Learn to trust the energy that is tossed at you, not the unfilled words or the vacant actions that are just for show. *"I found the key to happiness. Stay away from idiots."* – Morgan Freeman.

Never allow anyone who has not been in your shoes to tell you how to tie your laces. Even if they do have the same shoes, it's an undisputed fact that every person's circumstances and values are different. You will lose every ounce of contentment if you allow others to define what standards you should live by. Life will always be complicated; never wait for moments to be simpler before you start living abundantly. Learn to find contentment in every season of life; otherwise, you will run out of time. The world is changed by your example, not by your opinion! So do not allow the opinions of others to derail you either. Do not permit society to have influence over you to take you back to a reactive and uncertain version of yourself when you have laboured to become a better person to live by your true values. Remain true to your values. Be emotionally intelligent so you can be in a sound state of mind to make better choices. Living your own convictions is where contentment stems from. Peace is how you measure success.

When you feel overwhelmed, the way you react can make things worse. Unravel your common, self-sabotaging mistakes and how to avoid them:

- Stop enforcing the illusion that you do not have time for actions that may help you. Stop waiting for an ideal moment, and do something to help yourself immediately, such as finding a coach, taking time out, or spending quality time with a friend.

- Be realistic and create positive patterns. You cannot use your unconscious mind all the time. It's an irrational expectation to be focused all the time. Try taking a walk and letting your mind drift and see what clarifications arise; step away from the drama and allow yourself the psychological care to breathe.

- Do not interpret feeling overwhelmed as a limitation. Refrain from being difficult on yourself. Replace self-criticism with compassionate self-talk. Avoid overanalysing the situation.

- Pay attention to your default reactions, your customary responses, traditional methodologies, and conventional defences. Understand what your strengths are and use them to your advantage.

- Be acutely aware of your reaction to withdraw from your support system. Instead, seek ways to connect with people, especially when you have limited emotional energy.

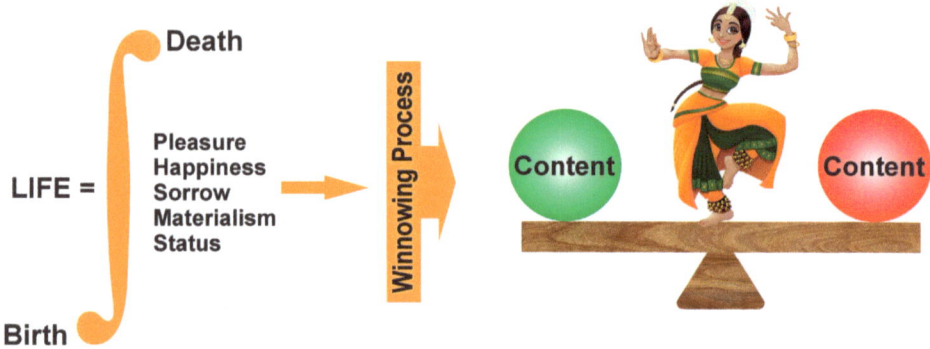

The Contentment Process

Finding the Balance to Contentment

Finding contentment throughout life involves a mindful examination of experiences from birth to death. It requires understanding that pleasure and happiness are often fleeting, while deeper fulfilment comes from embracing both joy and sorrow. By recognising the transient nature of materialism and societal status, we can shift our focus to meaningful relationships, personal growth, and inner peace. The *"winnowing process"* involves cultivating gratitude, practising self-reflection, and prioritising values that resonate with our authentic selves. Ultimately, contentment emerges when we harmonise our desires with acceptance, leading to a richer appreciation of life's journey, regardless of external circumstances. Contentment is a fine balance of acceptance.

People make irrational decisions daily only because they assume they will avoid losing something. Refrain from purchasing things you did not require simply because you feel you will miss out on a sale. You cannot be real about your own life, so you resort to throwing rocks at how others live. You decline opportunities because you are too afraid to take a plunge into the unknown – you are strapped to your comfort blanket. Making the foolish mistake of keeping busy, and if busyness means achievement, time is of the essence. Spend it on what matters. Failure to expand your horizon will leave you standing in a cave forever. Become conscious about how fear affects your narrative. Understand the limitations you place on yourself to reach your potential for progress, happiness, fulfilment, and contentment. *"Be content with what you have. Rejoice in the way things are. When you realise there is nothing lacking, the whole world belongs to you."* – Lao Tzu.

Rationalisation is the action of attempting to explain or justify behaviour or an attitude with logical reasons, even if these are not appropriate in accordance with the dictionary. Have you ever indulged in rationalisation? Visceral memory to plead your case and why you did what you did. This comes in torrents when you have done something incorrect, yet when you are living a lavish life and doing a conscious act of realisation, you are rarely strangled into submission of why. The social cost of hindsight ought to come to us regardless of whether we are at the top or bottom of the ladder. Many live their lives with the attitude of anything that floats their boat. Does your contentment register recognise others in your balanced or unbalanced equation of life? Most of us spend copious time traversing through charted and uncharted waters, only to discover that paradise is not what, where, who, why, and how you perceive it to be.

"Martin Seligman is a pioneer of Positive Psychology. He uses the scientific method to explore why happy people are happy. Using exhaustive questionnaires, Seligman found that the most satisfied, upbeat people were those who had discovered and exploited their unique combination of 'signature strengths,' such as humanity, temperance, and persistence. This vision of happiness combines the virtue ethics of Confucius, Mencius, and Aristotle with modern psychological theories of motivation. Seligman's conclusion is that happiness has three dimensions that can be cultivated: the Pleasant Life, the Good Life, and the Meaningful Life."

Even if you unravel all three dimensions of happiness, we have gleaned that happiness does not constitute contentment. You cannot dwell with a hermetically sealed illusion that contentment will find its way to you. Contentment is a proactive approach. Society has presumed to crack the code.

WORK HARD ⇨ CARVE A FINE LIFE ⇨ LIVE HAPPILY EVER AFTER

This is a myth. Many who have reached the peak of their game are not happy and seeking something substantial to quench their thirst. Ultimately, success is defined by you – the individual who knows without a shadow of a doubt if your heart's content regardless of all the noise that is present in your life. You align with your true values instead of hustling to the beat of the world.

"A fan and entertainment industry worker, Brian Lord, spoke about a prerequisite in Robin Williams' contract that required the production to hire homeless people to work on the film. The document also contained food specifics and other requests from the actor. The ever-creative Robin Williams also saw the opportunity to make a difference in the lives of the poor, and he took it. Although Brian and Robin never officially worked together, the document was in Brian's possession. The kindness and love that Robin personified were evident in his unusual request. Brian says, 'He actually had a requirement that for every single event or film he did, the company hiring him also had to hire a certain number of homeless people and put them to work.' During Robin's entire career, he helped approximately 1520 homeless people."

Robin Williams had a sensational career, a man with a great heart. He ticked all the boxes to acquire happiness. Robin found his contentment in addressing the burdens of the homeless souls. He could have chosen to bask in his glory, but he conjured up a contract to ensure he helps others as well. He was not just working hard to soar to the top. Every person has gone through some element of trauma in life, some are homeless, and it may not be your burden to usher forth a remedy to this. People like Robin Williams took the responsibility to help in some small way. Growth is understanding that you cannot change the whole world, but you can change yourself to impact the world in a profound manner. This is how the aroma of hope is created, and it unleashes contentment to both the giver and receiver. How you stride with the shattered expresses more than how you convene with the prosperous.

Relearn how to live life. Break up with assumptions, hone in on instincts to make a material difference, challenge the habits that you are set in, and constantly open your mind to new avenues that may glide you to a path of contentment. Genuine contentment does come with a refill. It is replenishing when you are aligned with the values that sustain you. The cost of inaction would have probably cost Robin his contentment. He did not ignore the burden of being an emotional pillar. Instead, Robin recognised empathy as part of his work. When you practice universal compassion, then you lead by example. There is no exercise better for the heart than reaching down and lifting people up. When you give cheerfully and accept gratefully, everyone is blessed. You have not lived today until you have done something for someone who can never repay you. You may have financial goals that you hope will lead you to contentment: do you save after you spend? Or spend after you save? Perhaps you go broke trying to look rich. Only you can define the tapestry that creates contentment for you.

Your life unveils the unquestioning commitment, discipline, fairness, goals, and tenacity to persevere. Inch by frozen inch, you create your life and contentment. Nothing is quaint or irrelevant. It all adds to the narrative. Your extraordinary deeds will pave the way. When the odds are stacked up against you, it will expose the brittle state of the world and what you are really made from. When you set your own standards to accomplish what brings you contentment, then you must fight against the unacceptable on contemporary platforms of life. This is not a time to retreat or acquiesce but rather to focus on what brings you contentment. The best way to support others is not to cheer them up. It is to show up. When the odds are mounted up against you, watch who brings you encouragement. Never be disillusioned when people reveal who they sincerely are; be thankful that you now have the knowledge to move forward with no misconceptions, and you can spend your energy on what matters.

The ultimate purpose of life is to make informed decisions. *"Everything can be taken from a man but one thing: the last of human freedoms – to choose one's attitude in any given set of circumstances, to choose one's own way." –* Viktor Frankl. Granted that you have the freedom to choose, then contentment is in your hands. Prospection is also in your hands, the act of looking forward in time or considering the future. Never exchange any distraction for what you want to accomplish in the future. Analyse your habits and ensure whatever entertains you now will pay dividends in the future. It is challenging to build with those who are not assisting you to carry the bricks; however, the onus is upon you to make it possible. Refuse to allow moments of vulnerability to disrupt your determination.

"King Richard is a 2021 American biographical sports drama film directed by Reinaldo Marcus Green. The film stars Will Smith as Richard Williams, the father and coach of famed tennis players Venus and Serena Williams (both of whom served as executive producers on the film), Richard Williams lives in Compton, California, with his wife Brandy, his three stepdaughters, and his two daughters, Venus and Serena. Richard aspires to turn Venus and Serena into professional tennis players; he has prepared a plan for success since before they were born. Richard and Brandy coach Venus and Serena daily, while also working as a security guard and a nurse, respectively. Richard works tirelessly to find a professional coach for the girls, creating brochures and videotapes to advertise their skills, but has not had success.

One day, Richard takes the girls to see coach Paul Cohen, who is in the middle of practicing with John McEnroe and Pete Sampras. Despite his initial reservations, he agrees to watch the girls practice, and is impressed. However, the Williamses cannot afford professional coaching, and Paul refuses to coach both girls for free; he selects Venus to receive his coaching, while Serena continues to practice with Brandy. Paul encourages Venus to participate in juniors tournaments. She quickly finds success, but Richard stresses to Venus and her sisters that they should remain humble despite their success. At one of Venus's tournaments, Serena also signs up to play, unbeknownst to Richard. As both girls continue to succeed, the family is treated as outsiders among the predominantly white, upper-class competition.

Richard meets with high-profile agents, but, fearing that his daughters will be taken advantage of, pulls them out of the junior circuit entirely. Paul warns him that his decision will destroy the girls' chances to turn pro, but Richard stands firm, firing Paul as a coach. Coach Rick Macci travels to California to see the girls play. Impressed, he takes the girls on, and the family relocates to Florida to train at his facility. Richard surprises Rick by reiterating that the girls will not play juniors, instead training and attending school like normal little girls. In the ensuing three years, questions arise from the media and from Rick about Richard's strategy with the girls and his desire for media exposure. Venus tells Rick that she wants to turn pro. Richard reluctantly agrees, but later reneges, worrying that she will suffer a similar fate to Rick's pupil Jennifer Capriati, who is allegedly suffering from burnout and has been arrested for drug possession. The decision strains Richard's relationships with Venus, Brandy, and Rick.

After an argument with Brandy, he reconciles with Venus, agreeing to let her play in the upcoming Bank of the West Classic in Oakland, California. Before the tournament, the family meets with a Nike executive, who offers them a major sponsorship deal worth 3 million dollars. Rick urges them to accept, but the family collectively agrees to decline, believing that once Venus begins to play, she will attract more lucrative offers. Venus initially struggles in her first professional match against Shaun Stafford, but eventually triumphs. She comes in as a heavy underdog in her next match against top-seeded Arantxa Sánchez Vicario. Venus takes the first set and leads in the second before Vicario takes an extended bathroom break, an apparent act of gamesmanship. Sánchez Vicario recovers to win the second set and the match. Richard and Brandy comfort a dejected Venus, telling her to be proud. As the family leaves the stadium, a large crowd of supporters is waiting to cheer her on, and Rick tells Richard that several major shoe companies are anxious to meet with Venus.

An epilogue reveals that nine months later, at the age of 15, Venus would sign a contract with Reebok for $12 million (equivalent to $22 million in 2021). She would go on to win Wimbledon five times and become the first African American woman to be ranked number one in the world during the Open Era. Serena, who joined Venus as a professional two years later, would become a 23-time Grand Slam champion and considered by many to be the greatest female player in tennis history."

Richard certainly planned for contentment, a plan before his daughters were born. His perseverance and crucial planning are etched in history. You do not reach the top by sheer luck. Richard Williams defied the world when they mocked him about his daughter's playing tennis, let alone becoming world champions. The benefits of contentment are in the fabric of what you say yes to, why you say no, and how you endure despite all odds. Express your feelings in a fashion that fully matches your experience, remembering what brings you long-term contentment. Only create contracts and agreements that invite your welfare to the table and contribute to your contentment. Purge out defensive behaviours and become innovative by producing results that move you towards your goal and, eventually, your contentment. Commit to reveal and not conceal by expressing your authentic experiences, even under duress. Make clear and direct requests. Richard Williams models this to us in an impeccable example. Richard paints a vista to us about the true meaning of working ahead of the curve.

Humans indulge in all sorts of activities that allow them to become their ideal selves. It's a perpetual pursuit of fulfilling your idyllic self that grants you contentment, regardless of superficial pleasures or pain, regardless of positive or negative emotions. This is why some people are happy in warfare, and others are sad at a wedding party. Hence, why some are enthusiastic about work and others dislike celebrations. Finishing the marathon is not what makes you content; instead, achieving a complex long-term goal does. You get to define what success will bring you contentment, and what matters is not that we accomplish each of these plateaus of success but that you constantly move towards them, day after day, month after month, year after year. The plateaus will come and go, and you will continue following the path that will lead you to the depths of contentment.

With the progression of time, you will be able to identify what and who delivers contentment in truckloads or tipped out with a teaspoon to you. Endurance will call on you, and therein you will discover contempt or satisfaction. It will prompt you to realise that worthy things take time to come to fruition and thus develop deliberately and consistently. Peace will show up uninvited and prompt you to be reminiscent and persist to be composed through the storms of life, irrespective of the chaos encompassing you. Resilience will rock up and demonstrate to you that brighter seasons are ahead. Humility will sway in and convince you that you can achieve all things, not by your strength but by the strength of Christ. Compassion will ignite in your heart and punctuate you to be placid, sympathetic, and considerate towards yourself and others. Confidence will settle in and recite to you. Accept yourself and embrace your idiosyncrasies. Motivation will unleash itself and compel you to redirect your attention to what matters. Liberty will release itself and recap to you that you control your destiny. Love will chase you down and confirm to you that unconditional love dwells within you. Love who you are, and others will find you.

In 2014, I travelled to New York; on 28 August, I watched Serena Williams play tennis on a hard court. There were millions of people at the US Open. The event itself was surreal. Watching Serena in her professional stride seemed like she was a superhuman. Her story above reveals that we all have opportunities to grow something profound. Richard, her father, was not content with the default options, so he changed the narrative. Not everyone can frankly answer to being content. The culture of contentment demands that you dig deep and look at all aspects of your life to make meaningful changes. Master your mind. This is where you will win and lose battles. This is the locus where you are empowered to make choices and take strategic actions that align with who you are and what you want in life.

The benefits of being content extend beyond having a smile on your face. Being content plugs you with constructive emotions, supports your self-esteem, and promotes your well-being:

Nurture Healthier and Stronger Relationships
When you are content, you have greater self-awareness and recognise how to communicate your emotions and thoughts. This improves your relationships because you know how to listen to others, navigate conflict, and show your appreciation. You experience less stress. Stress is a key predictor of life satisfaction. The less stress you have, the greater your contentment and well-being. Being content shows you what's meaningful to you, which includes your health. Your health can become your top priority, and it's easier to remain at peace and experience less worry or

stress. You have better sleep hygiene: When you are satisfied with your life, it's easier to get a good night's sleep. Research has found that good sleep hygiene correlates with sustained attention, clear thinking, and emotional regulation. Sleep is when your body recharges and works to fight illnesses, so your physical health is better because of how you sleep.

Benefits of Contentment
For the Individual:

- *Mental Well-being:* Contentment reduces stress and anxiety, fostering a positive mindset.
- *Increased Resilience:* A content individual is better equipped to handle challenges and setbacks.
- *Enhanced Relationships:* Contentment promotes empathy and understanding, leading to stronger interpersonal connections.
- *Improved Health:* Lower stress levels can lead to better physical health and longevity.

For the Community:

- *Stronger Social Bonds:* Content individuals contribute to a more cohesive community, fostering trust and collaboration.
- *Reduced Conflict:* A contented population is less likely to engage in disputes, promoting harmony and cooperation.
- *Civic Engagement:* Contentment can motivate individuals to participate in community service and civic activities, enhancing communal well-being.
- *Supportive Environment:* A content community creates a nurturing atmosphere that encourages personal and collective growth.

Globally:

- *Sustainable Development:* Content societies prioritize well-being over materialism, leading to more sustainable practices and policies.
- *Global Peace:* Content nations are more likely to engage in diplomatic solutions rather than conflicts, contributing to global stability.
- *Shared Prosperity***:** A focus on contentment can foster a global culture of compassion and cooperation, addressing inequality and poverty.
- *Environmental Stewardship***:** Content individuals and communities are more inclined to protect the environment, promoting global ecological health.

Overall, contentment cultivates a foundation for individual happiness, community cohesion, and global progress. Always try to restrain your negative thoughts and rehearse the promises of God. Even if the applause may not be resounding, never wait for the gold confetti to unfold. Champion your victories. Perspective is the affirmation of fleeting happiness and lasting contentment. Never follow the storm; instead, focus on sprinkling happiness dust all over the world, and contentment will find you.

How content are you with...

- Have you allowed the death of a loved one to steal your contentment?

- Are you content with your boundaries and values, especially when society is not?

- Are you content with the view from the top of your success ladder and how you have impacted the world?

- Are you satisfied that you conquered the odds despite the unfavourable terrain? What would you change if you could?

Attaining Contentment

You know you have moved up the pecking order when your hotel reservation comes complete with a mattress menu, speechless but not sleepless. Perhaps contentment will follow swiftly. When you transition into the next realm, what accolades will make you the proudest? The money you acquired. The lessons that made you a better human being? The conscious choice to pursue neglected friends and family? The effort to cease quarrels? Located the time for what mattered? Took the high road to end resentments? Left no stone unturned to understand and be understood? Practice being more compassionate. Laboured to welcome strangers? Established boundaries with toxic people and organizations? Unconcerned about unforgiveness? Strive to protect your peace? You relearned how to build your dreams by rejuvenating yourself? Transcended your wounds into wisdom? Understood that certain separations are moral for progress? Revolved your mess into a message? You found life, love, and contentment?

Become the first responder to more extraordinary things by harnessing choices that give you contentment. Turmoil, lack of integrity, poor loyalty – the miserable condition of continual, unfocused attempts and erratic behaviour that invariably fails to produce the desired results. Who in their right frame of mind would choose this desired outcome as the destiny of the world? Yet here we are, living it by default with mainstream society. Some do strive to make superior choices, and what a breath of fresh air. The continuum of ego unleashes itself every time. You cultivate your confidence by the character you bring to the world. When you have a specific future planned and intend to live it, then your choices will align. When your character has no shame, then we all suffer. What have you always known but refused to accept about yourself? Has it disturbed your level of contentment?

In 2018, I dispensed the perfect antidote to myself: a Caribbean cruise, sun, sand, and pristine beaches. The extreme dilemma that posed was the choice between a piña colada or a strawberry daiquiri. All the critical thinking was parked off while I was in vacation mode. We anchored in Jamaica. I stood in front of Usain Bolt's statue to obtain the coveted photograph with the eight-time Olympic champion who dominated track and field sports. I was in his country, and it felt surreal. For some peculiar reason, the whole time I was in Jamaica, my mind kept going back to the Spanish runner, Ivan Fernandez, my subconscious mind was not on vacation. *"Spanish runner Ivan Fernandez Anaya is still receiving attention for a race he lost on Dec. 2, 2012.*

He was running second, some distance behind race leader Abel Mutai – bronze medallist in the 3,000 metre steeplechase at the London Olympics. As they entered the finishing straight, he saw the Kenyan runner – the certain winner of the race – mistakenly pull up about 10 metres before the finish, thinking he had already crossed the line. Fernandez Anaya quickly caught up with him, but instead of exploiting Mutai's mistake to speed past and claim an unlikely victory, he stayed behind and, using gestures, guided the Kenyan to the line and let him cross first. Tough decision, right? No. 'He was the rightful winner,' Fernandez Anaya said. 'He created a gap that I couldn't have closed if he hadn't made a mistake. As soon as I saw he was stopping, I knew I wasn't going to pass him. But even if they had told me that winning would have earned me a place in the Spanish team for the European championships, I wouldn't have done it either... Today, with the way things are in all circles, in soccer, in society, in politics, where it seems anything goes, a gesture of honesty goes down well.' Is winning all that counts? Are you sure about that?"

You may win the race, but you will never influence the world by trying to be like it. You may begin alone. You will fail alone. You might cry alone. You can win alone. All the lives that you touch in the process do matter. The Spanish runner Ivan Fernandez shows us that he is different. It cost him, but he was content and content at not cheating another human being. Success is revocable. Failure is not set in stone. Pluck is what will get you noticed. What behaviours do you foster and look the other way? These attitudes eventually seep into communities and hearts, robbing essential contentment. They mosey into your values, organizations, institutions, and systems, competing for narratives. Never let evil use you in disguise to win. In the wake of your fascination, understand right from wrong. Disagreeable parody will always knock on your door, but live with no fear, just in peace with the choices of your best life. Control how you respond to the things that are crafted to test you, and here in lurks your contentment.

Satisfaction is a guide to developing life's most important skill and a key to a meaningful life. It is not an easy task to find contentment. When you understand your basic values and try to align with them, you will uncover what you are content with, even if it costs you dearly. You can find a million distinctive ways to live passionately, forge bonds of friendship and love, enhance yourself, and defend those you love; it will mean jack if you cannot sleep comfortably. Contentment is something we should all strive for if we define it appropriately and have realistic expectations. That's because the research clearly shows that authentic contentment is correlated with better health and well-being, positive relationships, success in almost every life domain, and even longevity.

In between the cradle and the grave, you must earnestly unravel what invigorates you towards contentment. Standing against the backdrop of uncertainty can sometimes push you in a direction that erodes satisfaction. Learn at the feet of an experience like a teachable recruit. Managing both acceptable and unacceptable risks will lead you to a point where you are always presented with choices. Your expectations, decisions, and resolve will determine the outcome. Your contentment relies on your unambiguous requirements, benefits, principles, and purposes. Satisfaction will lurk within you, and you are not mandated to exhibit it to the world. Refrain from generating a genuine good imitation of having a life – this will rob you of contentment. Live out of your vision, not your history, and do not produce a career of being unhappy – every decision matters. Acumen, self-examination, revelations, and hard-won wisdom will concrete the way for you to be content. Life does not owe you anything back like people owe taxes. Understand that life will never be indebted to you. Live like you know that.

"Novak Djokovic has said he would rather miss out on future tennis trophies than be forced to get a COVID-19 vaccine. Speaking exclusively to the BBC, he said missing competitions, such as the French Open, over his jab status was 'the price that I'm willing to pay.' The 20-time Grand Slam winner was deported from Australia in 2022 after the government cancelled his visa in a row over his vaccine status. He said he had not spoken out in the media at the time – despite wanting to – as he wanted to respect the legal process and the Australian Open. The world's number one men's tennis player also said he should not be associated with the anti-vax movement but supported an individual's right to choose. He said he had obtained a medical exemption to enter the country to play in the Australian Open as he had recently recovered from COVID-19. However, the country's immigration minister, Alex Hawke, personally cancelled the 34 year old's visa on the grounds that his presence could incite 'civil unrest' and encourage anti-vaccine sentiment."

Yes, that's correct; *"civil unrest"* was on the precipice. Citizens of Victoria, Australia, were not content with double standards. They were mandated to endure prolonged lockdown conditions during the COVID-19 pandemic. They made themselves heard and expected their government to take heed of the facts: Granted that they were mandated to obtain COVID-19 vaccinations, then the same rule MUST be applicable to international tennis players landing in the state of Victoria. It is worth noting how all parties brought their values to the table: the local community, the international player, and the government. Each had the stance of what would satisfy them, and the hefty loss Novak Djokovic was content with even when he was thrust into a situation, and the community jumped up to voice dissatisfaction. In essence, the community, players, and the government had to delve into authentic contentment to march to a point of peace.

Life will always test you and push you further away from the anchors of contentment. The onus is upon you to stay on the path that will lead you to triumph. Who you become is more important than what you win. Novak Djokovic is the personification model for the world; he did not stray from his values. The Victorian community displayed what contentment looked like via their lenses, modelling to us always to find our voice and live it. Contentment is being assertive in a situation in which you previously would have been silent about. Contentment is requesting what you desire and not feeling negative for doing so. Contentment is establishing boundaries, especially when it is difficult. Contentment is making robust decisions because they are nourishing. Contentment is telling people how they can help you. Contentment is allowing yourself to feel without classifying your emotions as optimistic or pessimistic. Contentment is speaking about your concerns sooner rather than later. Contentment is communicating about your worries to supportive people. Contentment is liaising with organisations that can enhance the situation. Contentment is bidding for what you want instead of assuming that people will know what you need. Contentment is observing all the improvements.

The Australian bushmen's alarm clock is the kookaburra. What is your alarm clock to wake up to contentment? Life has a sublime vista only if you purposely create it. The human brain is an anticipation machine, and what you are keen on will affect your contentment. Remember that support is not always given. It's designed and crafted with your contentment constantly on the agenda. Be strategic about who you let into your life, personally and professionally. Do not underestimate the power of the influence of a single relationship. One person can change the trajectory of your life, and a single decision can change that trajectory. Brokering alliances under various factions will pay dividends. Understand what you build and who you connect with. It's essential to have realistic expectations. Do not expect to be happy all the time. It is expected to feel the full range of human emotions, from angst, defeat, melancholy, and annoyance, even enthusiasm, contentment, pleasure, and fulfilment, etc. Recognise that seasons will change in your life and be prepared for it. Do not focus all your energy trying to fix what is a passing season. Allow the season to teach and mend you.

You do not have to be loyal to those who are committed to misunderstanding you. Enemies pay little heed to your satisfaction, so craft your tribe with precision. People unearth their power when they find themselves after a game-changing moment when they have to face the mirror and ask themselves, *"Do I like what I see?"* It is challenging when you are going through a transformation, as you have to take ownership of the good, the bad, and the ugly to get that mysterious discovery and level up into the next stage of life. Begin with replacing criticism and comparison with acceptance and appreciation. Originate communication with yourself in kind and positive ways. Invent every opportunity to display respect for yourself by setting boundaries and prioritizing your needs. Design occasions to devote quality time to yourself. Develop trust in yourself by honouring your commitments. Surround yourself with a robust community of like-minded men or women who are there for you in the sound and challenging times. *"Rowan Atkinson was born in a middle-class family and suffered terribly as a child because of his stuttering. He was also teased and bullied at school because of his looks. His bullies thought he looked like an alien. He was soon marked as strange and became a very shy, withdrawn kid who didn't have many friends, so he dived into science, one of his teachers said. There was nothing outstanding about him. I did not expect him to be a brilliant scientist, but he has proved everyone wrong. Admitted to Oxford University during his days, he started falling in love with acting but couldn't perform due to his speaking disorder. He got his master's degree in electrical engineering before appearing in any movie or TV show. After getting his degree, he decided to pursue his dream and become an actor, so he enrolled in a comedy group, but again, his stammering got in the way.*

A lot of TV shows rejected him, and he felt devastated despite the many rejections. He never stopped believing in himself. He had a great passion for making people laugh and knew that he was very good at it. He started focusing more and more on his original comedy sketches and soon realized that he could speak fluently whenever he played some character. He found a way to overcome his stuttering, and he also used that as an inspiration for his acting. While studying for his master's, Rowan Atkinson co-created the strange, surreal, and now-speaking character known as Mr. Bean.

He had success with other shows. Mr. Bean made him globally famous, and despite all the obstacles he faced because of his looks and his speaking disorder, he proved that even without a heroic body or a Hollywood face, you can become one of the most loved and respected actors in the world. The motivational success story of Rowan Atkinson. It's so inspiring because it teaches us that to be successful in life, the most important things are passion, hard work, dedication, and never giving up, because without caring about our feelings and weaknesses. No one is born perfect. Don't be afraid. People can accomplish amazing things every day despite their weaknesses and failures. So go and do the best you can with the one life you've got."

You are entitled to your opinion. However, it is your responsibility to ground it with compassion; do not rip out someone's heart just because you can. Edit your perspective when new verification surfaces. Always ask yourself how you would feel if others had an unfair opinion about you. Does contentment make you, or do you make contentment? Remember that anything that leaves an ache in your guts that is the size of Africa will certainly not buy you contentment. Happiness and contentment create a formidable team, and thus, you will find contentment when you are a conduit to making others happy.

Life is about preparing yourself for long sweeps of rejection, dissonance, and discomfort. It would be best if you learned how to style compromises and opportunities in the wake of your daily contentment compass. Glamorising your reality without attaining contentment will lead you straight to struggle. Let go of people who are not ready to love you. This is the most challenging thing you will ever have to do in your life, and it will also be the most important. Stop having difficult conversations with people who refuse to think outside the box. Discontinue exposing yourself to people who are not interested in your presence. It is an innate reflex to do all you can to gain appreciation from those around you, but that's an impulse that steals your time, energy, and mental and physical health, and it erodes your contentment. When you begin warfare for a life of delight, significance, and obligation, not everyone will be ready to follow you there. It does not denote that you must modify who you are. It means you must let go of people who are not prepared to be with you.

When you are ignored, disrespected, overlooked, or mistreated by the people you give your time to, you are not doing yourself a favour by continuing to offer them your energy and life. The most valuable thing you have in your life is your time and energy since both are limited – the people and things you give your time and energy to will define your existence. Create a life where people who are tuned to you are allowed a seat at your table and watch how your contentment grows. You deserve real friendship, genuine commitment, and complete love with healthy, wealthy people. Deciding to distance yourself from harmful people will give you the love, respect, happiness, contentment, and protection you deserve. Some people will doubt you; others will challenge you. Some people will take your time without offering theirs in return. Some people will take you for granted and take your kindness as a weakness. Others will know you are in distress and add to it rather than soothe your soul, and none of it matters. What does matter is you! How you create a mindset and lifestyle to bounce back and drape your contentment on like it was never kicked out of you. Remember your WORTH.

"Cutting off a man's fingers would be an odd way to get him to do more work" – CS Lewis. How often we demand more of a person but strip them of the tools they require to accomplish the task. One of those tools is 'respect.' We are afraid to give this away in case we lose power after they do a better job than ourselves. A decent person empowers others. In doing so, more profound things are accomplished. Life is about raising other people to become who God intended them to be, in the place to which God has called them. You are not called to mock and judge a person based on their looks, attitude, or the million things that you are unaware of. Do not create a reaction based on the limited information you do have; you may derail a person for life. As much as you are seeking contentment, remember that your actions can rob someone of their contentment by your behaviour. Contentment begins in your own heart when it is planted and growing well in your mind. It will be discernible through your character. It will spread via your thoughts, deeds, and actions.

Does your life continue in relative peace; however, your hand is twisted by external forces? The febrile attention demands that you need to act a certain way. Risk aversion is on the horizon, but you would rather go with your gut feelings. The cost of inaction will leave you feeling remorseful, and that will puncture your contentment. Will you permit a perceived catastrophe to shape the future? Some love it, and others detest it, the glory of RETROSPECTION. Sitting alone and allowing your thoughts and actions to surface and paint a clear vista of your life. Emotions may escalate or find an equilibrium. Hard truths will glare back at you, and this is where contentment gurus are born, when you can see objectively and make better choices from your bad decisions or lack of coherent decisions. Vulnerability, evolution, ascension, new habits, and revelations in quietude and peace that are deeper than the absence of conflict will sprout; this is when contentment comes to visit. Welcome it and ensure it stays long-term.

We all shine differently in unique ways. You and I may see things differently, but it doesn't mean that either of us is wrong. Our journeys to happiness are as different as we are. Contentment will disappear when you strip a person for doing what they love and where they find contentment. Understand that we are all created differently, and no mould exists where one size fits all. Refuse to be mired by the darkness for so long. Find the light even when you are living in the spotlight – it can be very dark. Sometimes, the awakening happens when it is a little too late. The process may be slow, but it moves slowly towards the light. It is a light that refreshes.

"World famous wildlife expert Steve Irwin was named Australian of the Year – but the decision was overturned at the last moment, and the honour was handed to cricket star Steve Waugh. The stunning revelation is in a memoir by former Olympian Lisa Curry, who was chair of the National Australia Day Council at the time in 2004. The sudden switch came amid a media and public outcry after the much loved 'Crocodile Hunter' Irwin was photographed holding his then baby son Robert while feeding a croc at the Irwin family's Australia Zoo. The council, which awards Australia's most prestigious honour, and which had already told Irwin he would be the recipient, made the call to change tack in the belief he could nominate again in a few years' time. But tragedy intervened before that could happen when Irwin was fatally stung by a ray in 2006. In an exclusive interview with the Saturday Telegraph and other News Corp papers, Curry said she would have made a different decision today – and if it were possible, she would give Irwin the award posthumously. 'It was such a shemozzle that should never have happened,' she said. 'Today, I would have just said no, we are going ahead with it.

Sometimes, you do things to please people, to please the media or the public, and these days, I'd go No. This is what we are doing.' The person deserves it, and it's going to stand."

Steve Irwin was living a life that he was content with. Lisa Curry's remorse confirms that contentment eluded her for some time and probably still does. Contentment does not require us to lower our standards; however, it does call us to dissect the principles that society dictates to us. Never dwell in the lane of 'what if.' The failure to meet your expectations is not opposed to contentment. The act of failing and still appreciating the experience is a fundamental building block for contentment. Things go wrong. Mistakes are made, and negative emotions arise. Others see it as things going right, and society will still judge them for it. And that is acceptable, and we need to allow for variation in life – we are not clones. Negative emotions are necessary and healthy for maintaining a stable periphery. Learn to express them in a socially acceptable and healthy manner and direct them in a way that aligns with your values, also considering others in the equation – they matter as well.

Contentment is the process of becoming your ideal self, and you cannot reach this status when society and others control you like a puppet. Uncovering contentment is the most meaningful moment of your life. It will encompass pain, battle, even irritation and misery, yet most of the repertoire will bring you contentment.

Most of your life is spent chasing false goals and worshipping false ideals. The day you realise that is the day you really start to live and move much closer to contentment. Realise that you cannot please all the people all the time. Satisfy yourself and your loved ones. Everyone else is busy gratifying themselves. Combating the ageing process is like trying to catch the wind. Embrace it. It is a fact of life that your body will change. The same analogy is applicable to trying to change the mindset of others. Focus your energy on what aligns with your values and leave no stone unturned to pursue it.

Nobody is unflawed and justly content with their lot. When that sinks in, you are free of comparison and judgement. It is a liberating juncture. Not everyone will zoom into all the stuff that you do correctly; people have the knack to zoom in on what you do wrong. When that becomes well-defined to you, you will accomplish things for the right reasons. Never spend years regretting your choices – learn from them. Contentment and peace are the best medicine. Life is not a routine but rather a quest; even when you hit the bumps, learn to refocus your energy.

Examining and discovery are not simultaneous. They are two distinctly different facets of self-awareness. Examining or searching requires a conscious choice to look around and within. The reality of discovery depends on how much truth you can dabble with. When you introspect and make an investigation into the self, you will find there what you require or avoid, waiting for you to tame some emotions. You don't have to constantly go searching. Invent your stage, and everything will unravel for you. When you make a mistake, sometimes the damage is repairable. You may lose someone or something that means a lot. When this happens, you feel regretful that you keep thinking and blaming yourself repeatedly. This makes it difficult to move on; you become fearful and sorrowful in life. If you have made a mistake, look back to see what went wrong, how you could have done things differently, see if you can do anything to fix things, accept and apologise, and aim to improve with the lessons learnt. Contentment lurks under challenging terrains as well; you need to unravel it. Take small steps to grow a healthier and wiser you. Walk away from your comfort blanket, and this is where abundant living begins. Do not wait until someone is dead to value them. Tap into the benefit of a content life sooner rather than later.

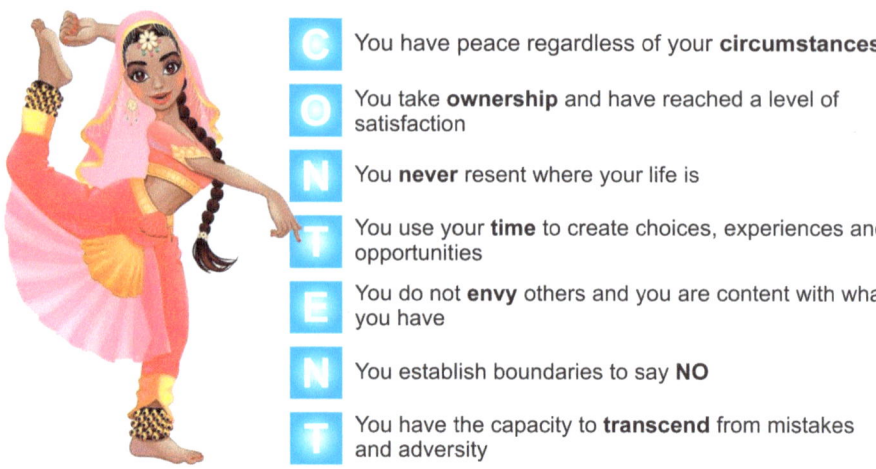

C You have peace regardless of your **circumstances**

O You take **ownership** and have reached a level of satisfaction

N You **never** resent where your life is

T You use your **time** to create choices, experiences and opportunities

E You do not **envy** others and you are content with what you have

N You establish boundaries to say **NO**

T You have the capacity to **transcend** from mistakes and adversity

The Contentment Dance

Contentment is a process; it becomes easier when you extend your process and refine it constantly. Purpose to not arrive at your grave with regrets. Construct incredible benchmarks for yourself. Live it, let people lose you. Walk away from million-dollar contracts that have no ethics, deteriorate, and rejuvenate – this is how contentment is unleashed, and the benefits lead to a better you. Living a content life is not a one-time achievement. It's something to incorporate into your daily life. You will not create a meaningful life by putting in work for several weeks. Contentment demands sustained effort, including strategies and habits that will become part of your routine. Record and share the things for which you are grateful. Practicing gratitude helps you focus more on your positive emotions and reminds you of what's meaningful in your life. Studies have found that sharing positive experiences with others amplifies positive emotions and leads to greater life satisfaction.

Stay true to yourself. Everyone finds different things meaningful or purposeful. That's why when you are living a content life, you remain your authentic self. Broaden your self-knowledge and understand what you love in life to stay focused on what's valuable to you. Keep your loved ones close. Keeping your friends and loved ones close improves your social health and ability to deal with life's challenges. Research shows that your support system helps you problem-solve, manage stress, and improve your self-esteem. Your people support you through your highs and lows. Your goals reflect your dreams and ambitions in life. They contribute to a more meaningful life – one where you feel satisfied with your accomplishments. Taking care of your physical and mental health is about more than just feeling suitable for a day. You are never set up for a long, peaceful future without a healthy mind and body. Dwelling on your past will not help you live in the present. But letting go of the past enables you to focus on the present and future.

In a 2020 interview, Mike Tyson said, *"You almost have to give your happiness up to accomplish your goals."* When you understand the benefits of contentment, then you can be willing to give up anything if contentment is what you strive for. Contentment is characterized by several key traits: gratitude, inner peace, acceptance, resilience, and a sense of fulfillment. To cultivate a habit and disposition that nurtures contentment in your soul, consider the following practices:

Pathways to True Contentment

Practice Gratitude
Cultivating a daily practice of gratitude can significantly enhance contentment. By focusing on what you appreciate in your life – no matter how small – you shift your perspective from scarcity to abundance.

Embrace Acceptance
Learning to accept your current circumstances, including flaws and imperfections, fosters a sense of peace. Acceptance doesn't mean resignation; instead, it's about acknowledging reality and finding a way to be at peace with it.

Cultivate Mindfulness
Mindfulness practices, such as meditation and deep breathing, help anchor you in the present moment. This awareness allows you to savour experiences without the constant pull of future desires or past regrets.

Foster Meaningful Connections
Building and nurturing deep relationships with family and friends can provide a sense of belonging and support, contributing to overall contentment. These connections often bring a deeper joy than fleeting moments of happiness.

Pursue Purpose
Engaging in activities that align with your values and passions fosters a sense of purpose. Whether through work, volunteering, or personal projects, contributing to something greater than oneself enhances contentment.

Limit Comparisons
In a world dominated by social media, it's easy to fall into the trap of comparison. Reminding yourself that everyone has their unique journey can help mitigate feelings of inadequacy and promote contentment with your path.

Reflect on Your Journey
Taking time to reflect on your experiences, lessons learned, and personal

growth can cultivate a deeper appreciation for your life. Journaling or meditative reflection allows you to see the richness of your journey, even amid challenges.

Embrace Mindfulness
Incorporating mindfulness practices into our daily routine can also be transformative. Mindfulness invites us to be present, acknowledging our thoughts and feelings without judgment. Techniques such as meditation, deep breathing, or simply taking a moment to observe your surroundings can help ground you in the here and now. This practice allows you to create a buffer against negative emotions and cultivate gratitude for the small joys in life.

Seek Connection
No journey towards contentment is undertaken alone. Building connections with others who share your struggles can be immensely healing. Whether through support groups, friendships, or community activities, fostering relationships offers not only solace but also shared wisdom. Often, we find that we are not alone in our experiences, which can provide comfort and encouragement.

Declutter Your Mind
Use tools like notebooks, calendars, and apps to offload information from your brain, make room for your mental resources to spark creativity and increasing problem-solving.

Prioritise and Focus
Multitasking reduces efficiency and increases errors. Focus on one task at a time and prioritise activities that align with your goals and purpose.

Declutter Your Environment
An organized physical space reduces stress and decision fatigue. Keep only what you need and be strategic about managing your possessions.

Embrace Decision-Making Frameworks
Simplify complex decisions by categorizing them and eliminating unnecessary choices, reducing the cognitive load. (Highly recommend reading *"Making Sage Decisions"* by Kelly Markey.)

Manage Attention Wisely
Attention is a limited resource. Avoid distractions like constant notifications and dedicate focused blocks of time to meaningful work.

Practice Strategic Information Consumption
Be selective about the information you consume. Limit exposure to irrelevant or overwhelming data.

Obtain Sufficient Rest
Sleep is essential for processing information, problem-solving, and maintaining focus. A well-rested mind is more organized and efficient.

Leverage the Power of Habits
Develop routines to automate repetitive tasks. Habits reduce decision fatigue and free mental space for higher-order thinking. Leading to greater contentment levels.

Freedom Through Self-Acceptance
True contentment is rooted in the ability to embrace yourself fully – imperfections and all. When you let go of the need for external validation, you release yourself from the constant fear of rejection. This shift in perspective is the key to unlocking authentic self-confidence and cultivating lasting inner peace.

Keep track of the external validations
Become aware of things that are out of your power that steals your peace and try to nip it in the bud.

Live in the Present
By grounding yourself in the present moment, you open the door to a deeper connection with life as it unfolds. Let go of the weight of past regrets and the worry of future uncertainties. Embracing contentment allows you to fully appreciate the now, reducing stress and bringing a sense of calm to your everyday experience.

Interpersonal Relationships
At its core, life is a web of relationships, and the quality of these connections plays a pivotal role in shaping your contentment. Prioritize relationships built on respect, trust, and mutual understanding. When you nurture these bonds, you create a foundation for greater harmony and fulfillment in your life.

Separation of Tasks
Recognizing which tasks are yours and which belong to others is crucial for maintaining balance. Focus on fulfilling your own responsibilities without the urge to control or manage what others must handle. This clear distinction not only minimizes conflict but also fosters healthier, more respectful relationships.

Contribution to Community
Engaging in meaningful ways with your community fosters a deep sense of purpose and belonging. When you contribute positively, you enhance your self-worth and strengthen your connection to others. This sense of value and interconnectedness can profoundly elevate your overall happiness.

Cultivate Courage to Be Disliked
Accepting that not everyone will like you is an essential step toward true freedom. The pursuit of universal approval only confines your authenticity. True courage is found in being unapologetically yourself, unshaken by the opinions of others.

Change Your Narrative
The stories you tell yourself shape how you experience life. By rewriting negative narratives into positive ones, you transform your perspective and empower yourself to face challenges with resilience. This shift allows you to create a more fulfilling, purposeful life.

Overcoming Feelings of Inferiority
Feelings of inferiority are often self-created, fuelled by comparisons that diminish your sense of self. Instead of measuring yourself against others, focus on your own unique strengths and potential. Recognizing your inherent worth is key to building genuine self-esteem and unlocking personal contentment.

Commit to Continuous Growth
Finally, commit to a mindset of continuous growth. Contentment is not a static state; it's a journey that evolves with you. Embrace the idea that every challenge is an opportunity for learning. Reflect regularly on your progress, reassess your goals, and adapt your strategies as needed. This proactive approach keeps you engaged in your life and encourages resilience in the face of adversity.

Attaining authentic contentment hinges on the distinct processes of self-examination and self-reformation. Self-examination involves a deep and honest reflection on one's thoughts, feelings, and behaviours, allowing individuals to understand their desires and motivations. This introspection highlights areas of dissatisfaction or discontent that may stem from unrealistic expectations or external comparisons. In contrast, self-reformation is the active commitment to change – embracing new perspectives, adopting healthier habits, and letting go of detrimental patterns. Together, these processes create a transformative cycle: self-examination reveals the roots of discontent, while self-reformation empowers individuals to make choices aligned with their true values. This journey not only fosters a deeper sense of fulfillment but also nurtures a resilient and authentic form of contentment that thrives regardless of external circumstances.

Achieving true contentment requires a shift in focus from the pursuit of fleeting happiness to the cultivation of lasting fulfilment. By embracing gratitude, acceptance, mindfulness, meaningful connections, purpose, and self-reflection, we can create a life that, while not always happy, is deeply rich and profoundly content. In this way, contentment becomes a sustainable source of joy, allowing us to navigate life's ups and downs with grace and resilience.

My Path to Contentment
As I reflect on my five decades of life, I see a tapestry woven from countless experiences, each thread representing a lesson learned, particularly about happiness and contentment. Because I grew up in a close-knit community, my early years were filled with the warmth of family gatherings, the laughter of friends, and the familiar embrace of shared traditions. But life, as it often does, led me on a journey far from that comforting environment – one that would teach me profound lessons about the essence of contentment. Immigrating came laced with the good, the bad, and the ugly, with eventual dollops of genuine contentment.

The Immigrant Experience
Moving to a new country was a daunting leap. The vibrant colours of my homeland faded into the muted tones of a foreign landscape. I left behind family and friends, each cherished bond now a memory tinged with longing. In the initial years of my immigration, I grappled with a sense of dislocation. The comfort of familiarity was replaced with the challenge of navigating a new culture, intimidation barriers, and a sense of isolation. It was a time when happiness felt elusive, like a distant star I could not quite reach. Even though I excelled and broke so many glass ceilings, to this day, I am not accepted because my colour does not meet the criteria. It is impossible to find contentment when you are constantly handed these cards.

Yet, in this unfamiliarity, I began to discover the nuances of contentment. Happiness, I learned, often relies on external circumstances – successes, connections, and fleeting joys. Contentment, however, is an internal state rooted in acceptance and gratitude. This realisation emerged gradually, often in the quiet moments of reflection that punctuated my busy days. I love the skin I was born in, and I had to seek my contentment regardless of society's vanity.

Lessons in Gratitude
One of the most transformative lessons came from recognizing the small, everyday joys around me. I learned to appreciate the beauty of a sunrise over the city skyline, the warmth of a stranger's smile, and the laughter of my new community and home. These moments, though simple, became the foundation of my contentment. I understood that while I may have lost certain relationships and familiar comforts, I could cultivate new ones in

unexpected places.

The practice of gratitude became my anchor. I started a daily ritual of listing things I was thankful for – big and small. This exercise shifted my focus from what I lacked to what I had. It was not just about surviving; it was about thriving in the present moment, regardless of my circumstances. I chose to be the bigger person even when others made me feel small; yes, indeed, sleep may have eluded me, but eventually, contentment reigned.

Building Community

Over time, I began to forge connections in my new environment. I sought fellowship with like-minded people and those who had nothing in common with me. I was a social butterfly and created a cosmopolitan melting pot to lean on and give to. Resilience and inspiration showed up. Together, we created a sense of belonging, sharing our cultures, our struggles, and our triumphs. In these gatherings, I found a new family – one built not on blood ties but on shared experiences and mutual support.

The friendships I developed were deeply enriching. They filled the void left by my absence from home and reminded me that connection transcends borders. In these relationships, I discovered that happiness often blooms in the soil of shared understanding and empathy. Contentment, I realised, flourishes in the heart of the community.

The Power of Acceptance

Another crucial lesson emerged through acceptance. Life, I learned, is inherently unpredictable. As an immigrant, the challenges I faced were often beyond my control – relocating, job instability, and cultural misunderstandings. Yet, I discovered the power of surrendering to the flow of life. Acceptance does not mean passivity; rather, it is an active acknowledgment of reality, a decision to find peace amidst the chaos. I also met many Judas characters who pretended to be friends but always had ulterior motives. Many still think I cannot see through their optics and fake loyalty; this is where I invite acceptance so contentment can stay forever.

This acceptance allowed me to cultivate resilience. Instead of resisting the circumstances that felt overwhelming, I learned to adapt. I became more resourceful, finding joy in the journey rather than fixating on the destination. Contentment, I found, was rooted in the ability to embrace whatever life presented, seeing each moment as an opportunity for growth.

How content are you with...

- Have you ever chosen to be second? How did it feel?

- Are you willing to lose so that you can remain aligned with your values?

- Have you ever judged someone harshly? How did that make you feel? How do you think the other party felt?

- Have you ever allowed society to control you?

- Do you have any regrets about a person who died?

Conquered Contentment

Shalom is a Hebrew word meaning peace, harmony, wholeness, completeness, prosperity, welfare, and tranquillity, and it can be used idiomatically to mean both *hello* and *goodbye*. It takes practice to attain Shalom in life. In 2014, I presumed that I had grounded confidence in the fact that I had acquired *SHALOM*... I was in the front seat of a helicopter flying over the city of Manhattan, viewing one of the greatest cities in the world. The vista of the New York Harbour from this vantage point was exhilarating, flying over the renowned Hudson River while catching aerial glimpses of how it meanders and eventually feeds the ocean and hovering around the legendary Statue of Liberty. I had just spent the morning at the US Open Tennis Tournament and was now heading to an exotic culinary experience at one of the finest restaurants in Manhattan. It was my 40th birthday, and life could not be any more amazing. My cup was full, and I was content until I stepped out of the helicopter and reality struck. The reality that unfolded on my milestone birthday is included in my book: *Don't Just Fly, SOAR*.

I gleaned from this lived experience that when life has me dancing like a willie wagtail bird on the mountaintop or helicopter to appreciate every moment, to relish it, to store it in my data bank of pleasant memories, and to capture the experience in photographs to remind me of the blissful experience. It is happiness, and it will not last forever. Reality will unravel when the helicopter lands. In this situation, it absolutely did. It took me three years to locate my contentment after this day. We all live in the meanders of emotions and validation of others. Contentment aligns your decision wheel to enjoy your happiness status and find the poise not to yell out or lose the plot when others derail your life. Life will never go according to the plan all the time. Choose not to place your self-worth in the hands of another person or even in that feeble – like button. Life will teach you that not all characters have a moral compass, so the onus is upon you to enjoy the fleeting moments of happiness and resolve to be content regardless of what follows.

Understand the roots of your overwhelming emotions and never allow them to steal your contentment. Recall your moments of happiness and revert to the photographs if you must, but certainly do not mix the experience of happiness and contentment. The latter is always in your hands, and you are the gatekeeper to your *shalom*. Explore ways to self-soothe and unravel what you need to, but never stagnate. Identify and address recurring stressors that deprive you of contentment. Have a plan to proactively develop coping skills to deal with situations that are beyond your control. Learn the art of resilience in the eye of the storm. Even if your complications seem endless, know that you can manage your life one step at a time. And reach contentment if you chase it actively. During the worst times in life, you will discover who cares about you – notice who will support you and stick around. Pay attention to those who just offer lip service or leave; this will give you the opportunity to grow in the abandoned space. Acknowledge the gift of absence by those who do not appreciate and respect your presence. It is where contentment will reign. Cut loose the hindrance.

The universe will isolate you so that you can discover your purpose. It could appear that you have lost friendships and relationships; however, uncovering your conduit, aspiration, true north, resolve, and real supporters in life is worth far more. When you find the fortitude to put up, then you will say a few goodbyes that will give you liberating peace, and there you will find your contentment. Remain vigilant, be present, always observant, heed more than you express, glance and question, be brave, and take that risk if you must. Walk away from those who choose never to celebrate you. Never regret the genuine stuff you did, even if people may never admit how much you have done for them. You do not need accolades from humans. The day you realise this, your contentment tank will flourish.

When I lived in regional New South Wales, Australia, I met a woman who shared part of her life with me. Her story profoundly touched me. She was in the prime of her life, living her best, when one unsuspecting Sunday, her life was stripped bare of so many securities that she took for granted. She was at church, where she came to fill up her contentment reservoir. Her son, a toddler who was two and a half years old, wandered off to the paddock, which drops to a mighty river. He saw water and took a plunge. He was escorted to the hospital. Fervent prayers went up for his life to be spared. Much to the angst of life and death, Jenny lost her son. How do you appease a mother who lost her baby prematurely? Was contentment even in Jenny's verbatim? Almost thirty years later, I was having coffee with Jenny and bantering, which confirmed to me how contentment never left her even in the worst storm of her life.

The garrulous media took hold of this tragic accident and turned it into a circus of blame and finger-pointing. Raucously, people questioned if God was in slumber and walked away from the faith. The whole community was shaken to the core. Jenny mentioned how her mother-in-law would bring all the newspapers with the printed propaganda to her doorstep and demand that she walks away from God because God allowed this incident to happen, and it was all His fault – in a season when Jenny needed unconditional support and love, the media, community, and family added more woes to her plate. Jenny was opposed to despotism and channelled her emotions and prayers. It gave the culprits continuing vigour to taunt her about the accident and God as if she did not have enough to struggle with already. Jenny persevered despite the hell and high water. Your diet does not consist of just what you eat. It consists of what you watch, what you read, who you follow, what you choose to let in, who and what influences you, and who you spend your time with. Contentment takes shape when you are strategically aligned.

Progressively, we still meet wounds vented as polarisation, and the difference in expressing this pain can divide rather than unite in a critical time. It sparks conflict rather than curiosity and healing. Unless humanity becomes mediators to assist in a combined dialogue, you are not going to be able to get the changes you need in the future and cultivate contentment. Catastrophe and conflict are considerable opportunities to learn how to change direction. If you take a fresh approach, you can define a path to contentment. It takes courage to be genuine, even when no one seems to understand you, and to do what is right and true for you. To struggle through barriers, to ignore the naysayers, and to allow God to direct your path. It takes the audacity to turn the other cheek, to step up and speak up, to serve the world even when you are bleeding.

It takes resolution to trudge along amidst the misfortune. It takes grit to fight resentment. Own your responsibility. You may not be responsible for your trauma, but you are responsible for breaking the cycle. Refuse to hurt people because of what happened to you. Choose to support, respect, and honour others if you want the same in return. Don't cry crocodile tears when you are cut off but refuse to acknowledge how you shunned the other person. What goes around will come around, and contentment will elude you. Be cognisant of what you dish out. You may need to swallow your own medicine. Life is superior when you understand that quality matters more than quantity. Refine your choices and relationships with excellence. Do not allow fairy tales to dictate a formula to you. Find your path that will lead you to contentment. Never subscribe to other people's prescriptions for life; find your sure foot.

The world requires more people with pluck, so it is necessary that YOU show up courageous. YOU can be the light and salt to humanity in the darkness. YOU can get knocked down by life but refuse to be reduced by it. YOU can resolve to dispense healing rather than more pain. View every trial as an opportunity to grow to a healthy plateau. Contentment was plastered all over Jenny's face when she took another bite of her toasted banana bread dolloped with fresh cream and strawberries. It was not the food that unleashed this. Tears welled up and escaped from her eyes when Jenny mentioned to me that she asked God why you took my baby, and God reassured her. *"I have your son here; he is safe and well in my care. This experience gave you the opportunity to question and abandon me or draw closer to me. Jenny, in the last thirty years, you have become so much closer to me. Your lived experience is an advertisement to the world. You are content despite your pain and loss. You have so much to teach the world."*

We all desire contentment but rarely accept the conditions that shape and contour us. If you had just 5 minutes to live, what would you do? We have all watched many catastrophes unfold on the silver screen where people grab their phone or pen and paper to write a message to their loved one or call to say their last goodbye. The fact is that we all have a finite time on earth;

do not squander your time and think you can make it matter in the last five minutes. Make every five minutes matter. Dish out contentment as much as you desire it. You serve it up by the character you choose to bring to the show of life. Sometimes, the price is too high, and these souls still find the silver lining.

Some people are even content to lose their life for a cause. Others get thrust into discontentment when they base contentment on things that cannot be controlled. Lack of contentment breeds' envy. This opens the floodgates to antisocial behaviours. To conquer life, you must understand how to be content. In our consumerist culture, where discontentment is promoted and material gratification is fortified, learning to be content can be challenging. Seize control of your stance if YOU are constantly under the notion that life will be better when you get married, buy a house, have a child, drive a Porsche, and the list goes on. Both happiness and contentment are not reliant on the procurement of any ownership. Contentment is your choice and yours to unravel. You cannot copy and paste – no two journeys are the same. Get off the comparison train; this is not a competition, and you and only you will understand what will bring contentment to yourself. Refrain from comparing your life with others.

Ride the wave of pride in the character that you fashioned and continue to develop. The rogue confusion is complacency. The meaning of complacency is **marked by self-satisfaction, especially when accompanied by unawareness of actual dangers or deficiencies.** Many make the default decision to get saturated in complacency and presume it is contentment. Both contentment and complacency are choices. They both stem from a combination of deliberate decisions, frame of mind, stretch in your school of thought, remediation in habits, and being aware of your thoughts, deeds, and actions, and the impacts they create. When your desire to leap forward ignites, then you will understand the power of contentment. There is a network of factors that will contribute to your contentment. This book is an endeavour to get you closer. My mission is accomplished if you are enlightened after this reading.

Silence is the impostor who knocks you off your game constantly and trades her with a cheerleader. Unearthing a genuine sense of contentment despite the commotion in your life is an achievement to be reckoned with. To achieve anything substantial in life, you need to build a firm foundation. You can decide what cornerstones you would like to use to make your stable foundation that will stand the test of time. Some of my cornerstones are loyalty, trust, honesty, agape love, and integrity. This creates confidence in me, the professional liaison, poise in the friendship, dignity with family, and grandeur with the love of my life, and it significantly paves the way to contentment. It takes a myriad of efforts to establish harmony and contentment. Perception equates to more than the quantity of lessons you gleaned. It manifests appropriately when it is soaked in your conditioning and natural responses – it shines when you regularly apply them; it tells the real tale. Acquisition of perspective is great, but the rubber hits the road when you uphold your perspective. Awareness, experience, and knowledge neglected is education wasted. Understanding, capability, and information that are ignored are development squandered.

Dismantling your self-love and self-respect will decompose your journey to contentment. When establishing a career, remember that no matter how much you love your job, if you do not create alignment with the number of hours you work, then contentment will fly out the window. Leave no stone unturned to fuel your contentment. Discuss and negotiate all terms and conditions that work best for you. Become acutely aware that avoiding conflict in any relationship is not a signal of stability but an indicator of a solemn malfunction. Healthy relationships require moments of authentic conversations, navigating through emotional turmoil and experiencing the chill in fractured harmony. Conflict serves this on a silver platter. It allows you to witness the unbridled truths, what's bubbling under the surface, and glean what the grey area looks like. Contentment has no 101 specifications, and it is vital to work out what you desire from each relationship and feel respected, seen, and heard.

As you navigate through life, YOU will discover the arteries and veins that will fuel your contentment. A simple aphorism to adopt for life... contentment is perpetually traversing away from the bedrock of the success ladder... the vortex of career... the vicissitudes of life... creating a beckoning bond with family... to establish memories with friends.... from friends to other friends... moving from city to farm... immigrating ... seeking love blindly... curated pleasure in the world... unconditional love... BLESSED with the gracious love of God... eventually death... in due course more death. In the end, only YOU get to decide what you fill in between these dots... carving your road to contentment one impeccable choice at a time. Regrettably, the most significant people in life can become foes in a flash. Coincidentally, rivals can become the vital people in your life without warning. The process hurts. However, when you accept it, it will improve your worth and sustainability, which will enhance your contentment.

Practice of escape, custom of denial, and application of reform. It is the purview of your life. I have been quenched by life many times. Contentment is conceivably the most coveted status of life. Contentment echoing with synchronisation of the most vintage hymns of joy, surging like a flashing star with twinkles of hope. Exhilarating like visions stimulated by choice and not chance, drenched by satisfaction. *"Contentment is natural wealth; luxury is artificial poverty."* – Socrates. How you maintain hypervigilance in good times as well as bad times will determine your balance of contentment. Some include tequila and salt to lemon to conjure up an impression for their sensors in a specific season. They learn to adjust to unfavourable circumstances as well. An art to flourishing...contentment. Life is brief; stop chasing the tail and chase contentment in all your relationships, in bed and the boardroom, and even in your chai and biryani. Hedonistic contentment will never deliver sustained fulfillment. The fact is everlasting happiness does not exist. You must find your contentment in the natural experience of life's highs and lows. Life essentially has two sides. Attempting to eradicate one aspect of life is ineffective. An accomplished life can embrace the positive and negative aspects of life and strategically grow from both.

In the process of attempting to fulfil these responsibilities (towards family, work, etc.), we forget we also have a responsibility towards ourselves – to be peaceful and happy. Our quest for happiness through others becomes dependent on how our relationships are, how our job is, and any other external factor that affects us directly in daily life. Our lives eventually become reliant on external situations. The tentacles of control slowly creep within us. Right from the time of our birth, expectations become an integral part of us. We are expected to do everything perfectly, and we don't give ourselves the liberty to learn from what we experience at each moment. Any role we play – be it as a student, employee, entrepreneur, parent, spouse, sibling, etc. – we are constantly trying to be the best in all spheres. Our focus is on becoming or doing everything perfectly rather than living each moment completely. We strive to put our stamp on being the role model for others in each of these responsibilities.

The ego presents another question: How do we live each moment completely if we do not like it and want to change it by controlling it? But isn't living each moment completely, without any judgment, the focal point of life? Can our life stagnate when we keep passing through different phases? How are we going to know that we dislike something before we experience it fully? We judge too quickly and want to change or move away from the situation, person, or thing we believe is unacceptable. *Memento Mori* is a Latin phrase that is translated as *"remember you must die."* While it seems gloomy, it highlights a potent fact of life's inevitable end. Thus, embrace each experience authentically and prioritize contentment regardless of your current, past, or future circumstances. The book of Philippians in the Bible is traced as the happiest book of the Bible, yet it was written in prison. Your circumstances do not determine your joy. Conditions do not map where you go. They merely reflect where you begin.

Astrology, emblems, culture, beliefs, traditions, religion, and people offer us glimmers of hope, but it is never quenching! Life cannot afford to lose any of her guardians, even when she has collaborated with the heart in such a manner that it never is permanently content. But she does donate moments of contentment that sustain us. The beauty is in finding these moments and stretching them, then capturing the formulae to retain them. Perhaps it is dressed up in the simplicity of walking barefoot on the beach as the sun sets, your hair is swept in the wind, and you have the fresh breeze hit your skin that is free of make-up. You drink in every moment. You are present, and you are content. Eventually, you let in the wall of graffiti, and it besieges your mind, entrapping you with no quick path to your great seat of contentment. The sanctuary of contentment cannot be found anywhere external. When you place the keys to your happiness in someone else's pocket, you will be dissatisfied. You cannot be complete, fulfilled, and content when you refuse to master this art within yourself.

The world felt different in the days following my brother's death. The sun rose each morning, casting light on familiar places, yet everything seemed muted as if a heavy blanket smothered the vibrancy of life. I would walk the same streets we once strolled, the echoes of our laughter haunting me. Each corner I turned brought memories rushing back and with them, an overwhelming sense of absence. The void he left was vast, an unfillable chasm that seemed to stretch endlessly.

Grief is a strange companion. It clings to you and wraps itself around your heart and mind, reminding you of the warmth that has been snatched away. I often found myself staring out of windows, lost in thought, the silence of my home amplifying the emptiness I felt. In those moments, it was tempting to succumb to despair, to wallow in the anguish of loss. But deep within, I knew I had to find a way to live with this pain – not to erase it, but to coexist with it. Even when sleep eluded me, I knew I needed to unravel something.

The months turned into years, and I noticed small shifts within myself. I started to realize that while my brother would never return, the love we shared was something I could carry forward. I began to look for traces of his spirit in my daily life. The favourite songs we had listened to, the movies we had watched, and the places we had visited all became a means of connection, albeit bittersweet. Each reminder was a thread that tethered me to him, a lifeline amidst the chaos of my emotions.

I began to summon a sense of conscious contentment despite my pain with trauma and grief. It was not easy. Each attempt felt like climbing a steep hill, the weight of grief pressing down on me with every step. I would sit in quiet spaces, close my eyes, and breathe. In those moments, I learned to embrace the silence, to allow the feelings of sadness and longing to wash over me without resistance. Instead of fighting against them, I welcomed them, acknowledging their presence. Grief, I realized, was not just about loss; it was also a testament to the depth of love I had for my brother. I still had to show up and be a professional in my day job. I still had to navigate envy unleashed by immature humans who could not deal with my prosperity in other facets of my life.

One weekend, I sat in Circular Quay, Sydney, Australia, where we made fond memories. I watched children running, laughter spilling into the air, and felt a pang of longing for my brother's presence. But as I breathed in the crisp spring air, something shifted. I noticed the colours of the leaves, the vivid hues glinting in the sun, and I felt a quiet warmth bloom in my chest. It was at that moment I understood that life, though forever altered, still held beauty. The world continued to turn, to create, and to breathe. Others were still happy despite my pain.

I began to seek out moments of joy, however fleeting. A walk in nature, a good book, a conversation with a friend – these small experiences became my anchors. I learned to celebrate the little things, each smile a reminder that while my brother was gone, life still carried the potential for contentment. I found solace in knowing that it was okay to feel joy again, to honour his memory by living fully.

As time passed, I developed a new relationship with my grief. I understood that the trauma of losing my brother would always linger like a shadow that followed me. But I also discovered that my heart could hold both grief and gratitude. Each day, I would take a moment to reflect on what I was thankful for – those memories, the laughter we shared, and the lessons he taught me. It became a ritual, a way of weaving his memory into my life rather than allowing his loss to define me.

In December 2024, I travelled to South Africa. The country that my brother lived. Reflecting on all the precious moments encountered in South Africa, one will stay with me for eternity...

After my international flight and the drive to my mum's home, it was after 10pm and just before I entered the home out of nowhere from the dark a huge butterfly zoomed in before me and danced in front of me.

I instantly knew it was my brother's spirit, and I said this is Jay and it fluttered and danced more and flapped its wings in front of me welcoming me and showing me, the way eventually leading me to the living room and then it danced and fluttered around from one end to the other. And I called out again to my family. This is Jay and the more I said it the more it fluttered and danced and eventually it flew right into my brother's room and remained there.

Wow, the words do not articulate my emotions. To have such an amazing welcome from another realm is beyond wonderment!

The butterfly often symbolizes transformation, renewal, and the soul's journey after death, making it a powerful and comforting image for those grieving the loss of a loved one. In many cultures, butterflies are seen as messengers or symbols of the soul's continued existence after passing. The idea is that the butterfly's metamorphosis from caterpillar to chrysalis and finally to its beautiful, free-flying form reflects the transition from life to death, and the possibility of peace and eternal life beyond physical existence. For someone mourning, seeing a butterfly might feel like a sign that their loved one is still with them in a different form, or that their spirit has moved on to a peaceful place.

Ultimately, it's a symbol of hope, offering a reminder that life and love continue in different, often unseen ways, even after someone is gone.

Peace and joy will always find you no matter what the circumstances are. Always trust your wings even when they feel broken.

There would be no quick fix, no magic moment when the pain would disappear. But with each passing day, I found that I could cultivate a sense of peace within the storm. It was not about forgetting; it was about integrating my loss into the fabric of my being. I could carry the love I had for my brother forward, transforming my grief into a force that encouraged me to embrace life more authentically.

I learned to sit with the discomfort, to recognise it as part of my journey. The void he left would always be there, a silent reminder of what I had lost. But in its place, I discovered resilience and a newfound appreciation for life's fragility. I allowed myself to feel joy and sorrow intertwined, knowing they could coexist as I trudged to the steep hill, unlocking my new shade of contentment.

In the end, contentment was not a destination but a practice. Each day, I chose to remember my brother, to honour him in the way I lived, and to seek beauty amidst the pain. Life would never be the same, and that was okay. It was a new path, marked by loss but also illuminated by love, a journey of finding peace in the echoes of what once was. Contentment unravels in mysterious ways, especially when we embrace the silence and dig deep for the treasure.

Kelly Markey

About the Author

Kelly Markey is a captivating wordsmith born in the fiery year of the Tiger. Hailing from a small town with big dreams, Markey's journey as an author is as bold and adventurous as the symbol that defines her birth year.

Kelly was born with a natural flair for storytelling. Her early years were marked by a fascination with words and an insatiable curiosity about the world around her. As a child, she would often be found immersed in books, weaving her imaginative tales that hinted at the creativity destined to blossom in her later years.

Kelly's writing reflects the spirited energy of the Tiger, combining strength, passion, and a touch of unpredictability. Her work spans across genres, from gripping page-turners that keep readers on the edge of their seats to heartfelt narratives that explore the complexities of human relationships. With a penchant for vivid descriptions and rich character development, Kelly's books come alive, transporting readers to worlds both familiar and inspirational.

In addition to her literary pursuits, Kelly is a fierce advocate for diversity and inclusion in literature. She believes in the power of stories to bridge gaps, foster empathy, and celebrate the unique experiences that make us all human. Through her writing, she strives to amplify voices that are often unheard and bring to light the beauty of our differences.

When she's not crafting tales or championing social causes, Kelly can be found exploring the outdoors, drawing inspiration from the wonders of nature. Whether hiking through lush forests or strolling along the beach, she finds solace and inspiration in the beauty of the world around her.

Kelly Markey's journey as an author is an ever-evolving odyssey, much like the dynamic spirit of the wild yet wise cat that influences her every word. With each new book, she invites readers to join her on an adventure, promising a literary experience that roars with intensity and resonates with the echoes of a life well-lived.

Kelly Markey **km**

CEO: Markey Writing Academy
Founder: Beacon of Hope Mission
Global Award Winning Publisher
International Bestselling &
Award Winning Author
Brand Ambassador:
Global Movement of Hope
Featured on New York
Times Square Billboard
kellymarkey.com

Celebrating Literary Excellence
Remarkable Milestones for 2024

"The Life of Jayandra," written by Kelly Markey and published by Markey Writing Academy, won the prestigious title of Top Book of the Year 2024 with IAOTP.

This remarkable achievement was further highlighted by the incredible milestone of having the book showcased on the iconic New York Times Square billboard – a true testament to its impact and reach.

The book, *"Echoes of Humanity,"* co-authored and curated by her and published by Markey Writing Academy, was shortlisted as a finalist for Book of the Year 2024 by KWE.

Having two remarkable titles in the spotlight in the same year is a testament to the dedication and creativity fostered at Markey Writing Academy and the international bestselling and award-winning author Kelly Markey. We invite you to celebrate this remarkable milestone with us as we recognize the hard work and passion behind these incredible works. Here's to a bright future in literature. Hats off to all her readers who put these books into action and changed the narrative.

In addition, it most definitely is a year of thriving – she was also nominated for the Kingdom Culture Advocate Award 2024 by KWE.

In New York, August 2024, Kelly was honoured with the Diamond Award of Excellence by The Beacon of Hope committee.

Lifeline Zululand nominated her for the Queen Book award in 2024, SURREAL for 2024. She has achieved and accomplished so much more in other years and will continue to THRIVE.

Markey Writing Academy

Kelly is the founder and CEO of Markey Writing Academy, her own publishing house that has helped others achieve their dreams of becoming successful international authors.

Welcome to Markey Writing Academy, where words transform into art and stories ignite minds.

At Markey Writing Academy, we are not just a publishing company; we are passionate about nurturing talent and crafting exceptional narratives that captivate readers worldwide. Whether you are an aspiring author with a manuscript seeking publication or a seasoned writer looking to refine your craft, our academy offers a tailored approach to meet your literary aspirations.

What sets us apart? Our commitment to personalized guidance, unparalleled editorial support, and a keen understanding of the evolving publishing landscape. We believe in empowering writers with the knowledge and tools needed to succeed in today's competitive market. From manuscript evaluation to strategic marketing advice, every step of your publishing journey is carefully curated by our team of industry experts.

Join Markey Writing Academy and embark on a transformative experience where your words gain resonance, and your stories find their audience. Let your journey to literary excellence begin with us.

Visit us at Markey Writing Academy and discover why your story deserves our dedication. www.kellymarkey.com

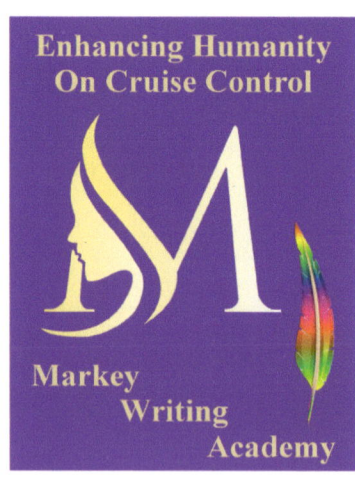

Beacon of Hope Mission

Kelly Markey is the founder and CEO of Beacon of Hope and Social Change Mission. This is a non-profit social enterprise. We invest our income into the global community. At Beacon of Hope, we are dedicated to uplifting narratives and empowering voices to inspire positive social change. We believe in the transformative power of stories to foster empathy, understanding, and action.

What We Stand For
Inspiring Change: We ignite conversations that inspire transformation and unity, challenge perspectives, and shed light on the human experience.

Promoting Suicide Prevention: We are committed to raising awareness and promoting initiatives that support wellbeing and prevent suicide.

Advocating for Mental Health: Through our publications, we champion mental health awareness and provide a platform for voices that encourage understanding and compassion.

Championing Social Change: Our collection of literature serves as a platform for underrepresented communities, highlighting issues that demand societal attention and advocating for justice and inclusivity.

Enhancing Literacy: We create awareness about reading and the doors it will open. We ignite the spark of HOPE that literacy, education and inspiration will unlock brighter futures.

Why We Do It
Guided by Kelly Markey's vision and dedication, our mission transcends mere publication. We aim to make a tangible difference in the world by fostering empathy, advocating for justice, and striving for a more inclusive society. Each title we publish embodies the ethos of social change, offering readers a glimpse into lives, struggles, and triumphs they might not otherwise encounter.

Join Me
We invite you to join us in our mission to empower communities and individuals. Together, we can embrace empathy, advocate for justice, and inspire change through the power of storytelling.

Sponsorship
Visit my website to sponsor our strategic goals.

Beacon of Hope Mission Forum

In an increasingly interconnected world, the need for hope and positive action has never been more critical. The annual International Beacon of Hope Forum serves as a vital platform to foster awareness, share experiences, and ignite change across borders. Here's why this forum is essential in our collective journey toward a brighter future.

A Global Gathering for Change
The Beacon of Hope Forum brings together individuals, organizations, and thought leaders from diverse backgrounds. This confluence of perspectives allows for rich dialogue on the challenges facing different communities. By highlighting local issues and global trends, participants can learn from one another and develop strategies that resonate across cultures.

Raising Awareness About Hope Initiatives
At the heart of the forum is a commitment to promoting hope-driven initiatives. By showcasing successful projects and innovative solutions, the forum helps to inspire others to act in their communities. This exchange of ideas is crucial for fostering a culture of hope that transcends geographic boundaries.

Empowering Voices and Sharing Stories
Every participant at the forum has a unique story to tell. By providing a platform for these narratives, we amplify the voices of those often unheard. Sharing personal experiences not only humanizes the issues we face but also builds empathy and solidarity among attendees. This connection is essential for cultivating a global community dedicated to making a difference.

Fostering Collaboration and Partnerships
The forum is more than just a series of talks; it's a launchpad for collaboration. By facilitating partnerships between organizations, businesses, and governments, we can leverage resources and expertise to tackle pressing challenges. The collective power of united efforts can lead to impactful, scalable solutions that bring hope to even the most vulnerable communities.

Highlighting the Role of Education and Awareness

Education is a cornerstone of empowerment. The forum emphasizes the importance of spreading knowledge about critical issues, from suicide prevention to social justice. By educating participants and the broader public, we can cultivate informed advocates who are equipped to inspire change in their communities.

Inspiring Action and Commitment

The goal of the Beacon of Hope Forum is to inspire action. Whether it's through advocacy, volunteering, or donating, participants leave with a renewed sense of purpose. By fostering a sense of accountability and commitment, we can transform hope into tangible outcomes.

Beacon of Hope Awards

The International Beacon of Hope Forum is not just an event; it's a movement. By gathering diverse voices and fostering collaboration, we aim to illuminate pathways of hope around the world. As we share stories, inspire action, and build connections, we take vital steps toward creating a future where hope thrives in every corner of the globe. Together, we can turn awareness into action and dreams into reality.

The Beacon of Hope Committee honours people from around the world who are proactive in being a beacon of hope to the world with a Beacon of Hope Award.

Michelle Jewlal: Beacon of Hope Award for Strategic Business Discretion

Loschinee Naiker: Beacon of Hope Award for Community Stewardship with Distinction

 Faye Marks: Beacon of Hope Award for Poetic Justice and Mental Health Awareness Excellence

Top Book of the Year

In this poignant narrative that delves into the profound journey of Jayandra, a soul grapples with the complexities of existence and the resolute determination to find meaning.

Through eloquent prose and heartfelt introspection, the author, Kelly Markey, masterfully weaves together themes of resilience, hope, and the human spirit's indomitable will.

Recognised for its profound impact and literary brilliance, *"The Life of Jayandra"* has captured hearts worldwide, earning the prestigious title of Top Book of the Year 2024 – IAOTP.

Now, witness its powerful message illuminated on the iconic New York Times Square Billboard, a testament to its enduring significance and universal acclaim that mandates change.

Join Kelly Markey on a transformative odyssey that transcends boundaries and resonates deeply with readers everywhere. Embrace a narrative that not only compels us to introspect the suicide landscape but also enlightens and invites you to ponder life's profound questions and celebrate the triumph of the human spirit.

An exceptional tribute to Jayandra…gone too soon but leaving a PROFOUND LEGACY ♥

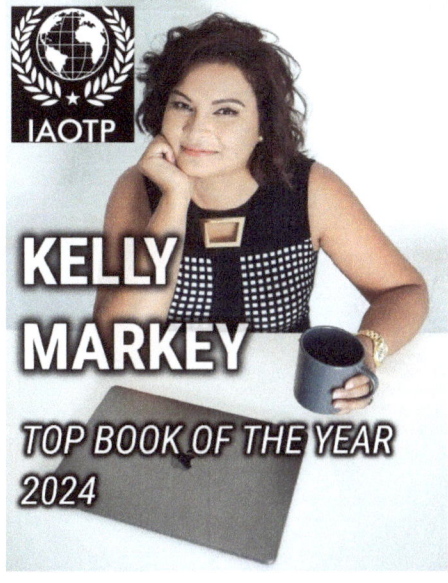

Featured on the New York Times Square Billboard

I prefer to have my brother here rather than this book. Yet this is the reality, and this book has begun the great work for reform on the taboo topic of suicide.

It's no small feat to be featured on the New York Times Square Billboard! WOW, thank you, God. Romans 8:28, *"And we know that all things work together for good."*

Jayandra, your absence gets louder and longer, my sweet brother, but something profound is prevailing in the void.

I am overwhelmed with gratitude for the incredible support and enthusiasm as I was featured on the New York Times Square Billboard. It was truly a once-in-a-lifetime milestone, and sharing that moment with others, whether in person or online, made it even more special.

Your encouragement and presence – whether cheering me on in New York or tuning in from afar – meant more to me than words can express. Thank you for being a part of this epic experience and for making it a memory I will cherish forever. With heartfelt thanks.

Acknowledgments

I want to express my heartfelt gratitude to my family and friends, whose unwavering support and love have helped me discover my level of contentment in every season of life. Your encouragement has been invaluable on this journey.

A special thank you to Dr. Stephanie Fletcher-Lartey, whose beautiful foreword set the tone for this book. Your insight and wisdom have enriched these pages.

In addition, I would like to extend my appreciation to Stephanie Tranquille and Janice Morris for their inspiring book acclaims for exploring the themes of this work.

My sincere gratitude to the team at Markey Writing Academy for the impeccable professional services that brought this book to life as a world-class product.

Heartfelt thanks to my professional editor, Cyrene. Her skill set is greatly appreciated.

To my readers, thank you for embarking on this journey with me. Your willingness to engage with these ideas is what makes this book meaningful. I encourage you to leave a review on @Goodreads, as your feedback will help others tap into this profound well of wisdom.

With gratitude,

Reference

Introduction

1. The origin of integrity, Merriam Webster, The Merriam Webster Dictionary, 11 ed, Springfield, 2004.

2. Quote: *"Employ . . . for."* Socrates 399 – 470 BC Greek philosopher, scholar and teacher.

3. Quote: *"To . . . going."* Ralph Waldo Emerson, poet and philosopher.

The Gist of Life

4. Reference to quote: *"Our . . . matter."* Francis Chan, online.

5. Psalm 37: 4 – 4, Zondervan, The Holy Bible, New International Version, USA, Harper Collins, 1973.

6. Quote: *"Patience . . . Success."* Napoleon Hill.

7. Reference to Royal Bafokeng tribe.

https://en.wikipedia.org/wiki/Royal_Bafokeng_Nation

8. Matthew 20:28, Zondervan, The Holy Bible, New International Version, USA, Harper Collins, 1973

9. Quote: *"You... defeated."* Maya Angelou.

10. Reference to Fiji date line.

https://chantae.com/international-date-line-taveuni-fiji/

11. Reference to Kobe Bryant.

https://wealthygorilla.com/kobe-bryant-net-worth/

12. Mention of Leban cheating Jacob.

https://en.wikipedia.org/wiki/Laban_(Bible)

13. Life of David Attenborough.

https://en.wikipedia.org/wiki/David_Attenborough

Superficial Satisfaction

14. The Gospel of Mark, Zondervan, The Holy Bible, New International Version, USA, Harper Collins, 1973

15. Quote: *"Life... delightful."* George Bernard Shaw.

16. Reference to hubris.

https://www.google.com/search?client=safari&rls=en&q=Hubris&ie=UTF-8&oe=UTF-8

17. Reference to Vincent Willem van Gogh,

https://www.britannica.com/biography/Vincent-van-Gogh

18. Port Arthur massacre, Australia.

https://en.wikipedia.org/wiki/Port_Arthur_massacre_(Australia)

19. Quote: *"It's… altitude."* Zig Ziglar.

20. Habakkuk 3: 17 – 19, Zondervan, The Holy Bible, New International Version, USA, Harper Collins, 1973

21. Suicide Statistics, Suicide rate, 2021

Complications to Contentment

22. Reference to menopause onset.

https://edition.cnn.com/2020/01/14/health/menopause-onset-sex-wellness/index.html

23. Quote: *"Both… parachute."* George Bernard Shaw

24. Journey Diagram, analysis and specifications by Kelly Markey and CorelDRAW illustration by Dave Markey.

Finding your Equilibrium

25. Reference to the brolga bird.

https://en.wikipedia.org/wiki/Brolga

26. Quote: *"The… stimulus."* Billy Graham.

27. Quote: *"Progress… anything."* George Bernard Shaw.

Habits for Satisfaction

28. Reference to Prince Harry's drinking.

https://edition.cnn.com/2021/05/21/world/prince-harry-oprah-drinking-scli-intl-gbr/index.html

29. Reference to Prince Harry's wearing a Nazi costume.

https://www.ladbible.com/news/prince-harry-netflix-nazi-costume-887753-20221208

30. Reference to Elon Musk's ultimatum.

https://www.moneycontrol.com/news/trends/rip-twitter-trends-as-employees-resign-in-hundreds-after-elon-musks-ultimatum-9558021.html

31. Reference to the term *"I'll be a monkey's uncle."*

https://en.wikipedia.org/wiki/Monkey%27s_uncle

32. Mention to Nick Vujicic.

https://en.wikipedia.org/wiki/Nick_Vujicic

33. Circle of contentment diagram, analysis and specifications by Kelly Markey and CorelDRAW illustration by Dave Markey.

34. Quote: *"Man… shore."* Andre Gide.

35. Excerpt from book, Kelly Markey, Don't Just Fly, Soar, Ultimate World Publishing, Australia, 2021.

36. Gratitude playing a key role in strengthening relationships

https://www.labmanager.com/news/gratitude-expressions-improves-cardiovascular-responses-to-stress-28210

37. Reference to Stephen tWitch Boss.

https://www.dailymail.co.uk/news/article-11545811/Stephen-tWitch-Boss-left-suicide-note-motel-alluding-past-challenges-death.html

38. Quote: *"Many… dies."* Elon Musk.

Quote: *"Every… it."* Tyler Perry.

Practice Prepares You for Success

39. Luke 2:7, Zondervan, The Holy Bible, New International Translation (NIV), United States. Harper Collins, 1973.

40. Excerpt from the book: Behrouz Boochani, *"No Friend but the Mountains,"* Australia, Pan Macmillan Pty Ltd, 2018.

41. Reference to William Shakespeare's book, Julius Caesar.

https://www.google.com/search?client=safari&rls=en&q=Brutus+our+falls+does+not+fall+on+our+stars+but+on+our+selfs&ie=UTF-8&oe=UTF-8&safari_group=9

42. Reference to Jim Kwik:

https://www.mindvalley.com/superbrain/masterclass

43. Prince Harry and Meghan stepping away from Royal duties.

https://www.vogue.com/article/prince-harry-meghan-markle-detail-why-they-left-the-royal-family

44. Quote: *"Competition… civilisation."* Peter Kropotkin.

45. Harvard study on your workday mental health.

https://hbr.org/2024/05/make-your-workday-work-for-your-mental-health?utm_campaign=hbr&utm_medium=social&utm_source=linkedinnewsletter&tpcc=linkedinnewsletter

Expectation Versus Reality

46. Quote: *"Never… good."* Unknown

47. Reference to Google.

https://www.theverge.com/2019/12/4/20994361/google-alphabet-larry-page-sergey-brin-sundar-pichai-co-founders-ceo-timeline

48. Reference to Andrea Bocelli. https://en.wikipedia.org/wiki/Andrea_Bocelli

49. How dopamine drives behaviour.

https://www.intoactionrecovery.com/how-dopamine-drives-our-behavior/

50. Matthew 6:25, Zondervan, The Holy Bible, New International Translation (NIV), United States. Harper Collins, 1973.

51. 2 Corinthians 11:23–28, Zondervan, The Holy Bible, New International Translation (NIV), United States. Harper Collins, 1973.

52. Reference to the 'falling man' during the September 11 attacks.

https://en.wikipedia.org/wiki/The_Falling_Man

Craft the Right Attitude

53. Quote: *"Our… wind."* Seneca,

54. Significance of wearing sindoor.

https://en.wikipedia.org/wiki/Sindoor

55. Search within diagram, analysis and specifications by Kelly Markey and CorelDRAW illustration by Dave Markey.

56. Reference to Kavaan, the world's loneliest elephant.

https://en.wikipedia.org/wiki/Kaavan

57. Quote: *"The… begin."* Tony Robbins.

58. Reference to American survey.

https://nypost.com/2019/12/02/most-americans-average-about-five-good-deeds-a-month/

59. Excerpt from book, Kelly Markey, Don't Just Fly, Soar, Ultimate World Publishing, Australia, 2021.

60. Excerpt from book, Kelly Markey, Making Sage Decisions, Beyond Publishing, USA, 2023.

The Correlation Between Happiness and Contentment

61. Quote: *"We… joy."* – Joseph Campbell.

62. Reference to cherophobia:

https://positivepsychology.com/cherophobia/

63. Statistics, Our World in Data, https://ourworldindata.org/happiness-and-life-satisfaction

64. Quote: *"The… nature."* Marcus Aurelius,

Benefits of Contentment

65. Excerpt from the book, Tony Thompson, *"Shakespeare the most famous man in London,"* Australia, Black Dog Books, 2009.

66. Reference to Sarah Jessica Parker, post from Instagram, 2022.

67. Quote: *"I… idiots."* Morgan Freeman.

68. The balance of contentment diagram, analysis and specifications by Kelly Markey and CorelDRAW illustration by Dave Markey.

69. Quote: *"Be… you."* Lao Tzu,

70. Three dimensions of happiness.

https://www.pursuit-of-happiness.org/history-of-happiness/martin-seligman-psychology/

71. Reference Robin Williams.

https://news.thehungersite.greatergood.com/dyr-robin-williams-films/

72. Quote: *"Everything… way."* Viktor Frankl,

73. Reference to the movie King Richard.

https://en.wikipedia.org/wiki/King_Richard_(film)

Attaining Contentment

74. Reference to Spanish runner.

https://www.usatoday.com/story/gameon/2013/01/19/ivan-fernandez-anaya-runner-loses-on-purpose/1847999/

75. Reference to Novak Djokovic.
https://www.bbc.com/news/world-australia-60014059

76. Reference to Mr. Bean, Rowan Atkinson. Retrieved from

https://en.wikipedia.org/wiki/Rowan_Atkinson

77. Quote: *"Cutting… work"* CS Lewis,

78. The contentment dance diagram, analysis and specifications by Kelly Markey and CorelDRAW illustration by Dave Markey.

79. Reference to Lisa Curry revealing why Steve Irwin lost the Australian of the Year award.
https://www.nzherald.co.nz/lifestyle/lisa-curry-reveals-why-steve-irwin-lost-australian-of-year-to-steve-waugh-in-new-book/73GBFEKQ2SEUQIGHGKJOO5LRLA/

Conquered Contentment

80. Meaning of Shalom. https://en.wikipedia.org/wiki/Shalom

81. Quote: *"Contentment… poverty."* Socrates.

www.ingramcontent.com/pod-product-compliance
Lightning Source LLC
Chambersburg PA
CBHW041218070526
44583CB00006B/169